OXFORD GOLDSMITHS
BEFORE 1800

OXFORD
GOLDSMITHS
BEFORE 1800

Ann Natalie Hansen

AT THE
SIGN OF THE COCK

COLUMBUS, OHIO

Library of Congress Catalog Card Number 96-85528
ISBN 0-9613491-3-1

Acknowledgements

Many diverse people contributed to making this book a reality. First I want to thank Katherine Duncan-Jones, Fellow of Somerville College, Oxford, for suggesting I have a look at the bursars' books of the ancient colleges which led to *Oxford Goldsmiths* growing from an intended article to a book, and the archivists of those colleges who gave me access to their muniments, as well as Simon Bailey, University Archivist, who patiently endured my many requests. I also owe a debt of gratitude to Timothy Wilson, Keeper of Western Art, Ashmolean Museum, Oxford, for allowing me to handle the ancient staves of the University and for his continuing enthusiasm for my research; to the staff of the Oxfordshire Archives, and to David Beasley, Librarian of the Worshipful Company of Goldsmiths, Goldsmiths' Hall, London.

Others who contributed to my knowledge were Ted East, former University Marshal; John Dobson, University Verger, who made it possible for me to handle the eighteenth century University staves currently in use; Albert Greenwood of Trinity College, for my visits to the vault containing the college silver, and Tony Matthews, Lord Mayor's Sergeant Macebearer, for showing me the City Plate in the fourteenth century vault under the Town Hall.

Last, but not least, I owe an enormous debt of gratitude to Dr. Helen Clifford, my erstwhile colleague, formerly Leverhulme Research Fellow, Department of Western Art, Ashmolean Museum, who opened many doors for me and was party to lively discussions over repasts at the Randolph.

Contents

About the Notes

All references to vital statistics of goldsmiths and members of their families are documented in the relevant parish registers and their transcripts in the Oxfordshire Archives unless otherwise noted. Copies are also in the Centre for Oxfordshire Studies at the Central Library, Oxford.

References to the Oxford Council Acts are abbreviated *OCA* plus relevant dates. These printed volumes of primary sources published by the Oxfordshire Historical Society over a period of years are as follows:

> H. E. Salter, *Oxford Council Acts, 1583–1626* (1928).
> M. G. Hobson and H. E. Salter, *Oxford Council Acts, 1626–1665* (1933).
> M. G. Hobson, *Oxford Council Acts, 1666–1701* (1939).
> M. G. Hobson, *Oxford Council Acts, 1701–1752* (1954).
> M. G. Hobson, *Oxford Council Acts, 1752–1801* (1957).

Vice-Chancellors' Accounts and Chancellors' Court Registers are in the Oxford University Archives.

The Sources

The City of Oxford is fortunate in having the Hanaster Books which begin in 1514. These large manuscript volumes contain the register of apprentices of all trades and the enrollment of freemen. Hanaster is a local term for freemen and may have derived from *Hanasterius* which seems to be the Latinized form of the Old German *Hansa, Societas mercatorum;* i.e., a corporation of merchants as found in Hamburg, Lübeck and Bremen.[1]

The Hanaster Books were kept in Latin until about the 1630s, but strangely, occupations were always written in English. When an apprentice was enrolled he was usually about fifteen years old. Included, besides the date of enrollment, were his father's name and occupation and his place of residence, and the name and occupation of the master to whom he was apprenticed, the length of the apprenticeship, and any other terms of the agreement. Like all such early records, there are unexplained omissions, and it is obvious that many of the earliest apprentices somehow did not make it into the Hanaster Books.

Next in importance are the account books of the old Oxford colleges, to be discussed in more detail presently. Also helpful are parish records, wills and inventories, and Petty Sessions records in the Oxfordshire Archives, the Vice-Chancellors' accounts and Chancellors' Court Registers in the University Archives, the Court Minute Books of the London Goldsmiths' Company at Goldsmiths' Hall, London, Sun Fire Insurance records at the London Guildhall, wills proved in the Prerogative Court of Canterbury in the Public Record Office, London, as well as various printed primary materials including the Oxford Council Acts, and *Jackson's Oxford Journal.*

---

[1] W. H. Turner, *Selections from the Records of the City of Oxford, 1509–1583* (1880), 23.

The account books of the colleges yield the most detailed information about the work of the Oxford goldsmiths. In most cases these records are known as Bursar's Books, but at Christ Church they are known as Treasurer's Disbursement Books and at Corpus Christi they are known as Libri Magni. More information is gleaned from the Buttery Accounts at Jesus, and at Magdalen the Bursar's Accounts were kept in Latin well into the nineteenth century. Brasenose has all the actual bills from every tradesman beginning in the seventeenth century in contrast to Wadham whose records have suffered from neglect over the years. Surprisingly, some of the richest colleges, for instance Merton, yield no information. For the most part as the years pass, the college accounts become more and more sketchy and more carelessly kept.

The amount of detail contained in these manuscripts varies enormously from college to college. Some of them throw light on other facets of college life. At Exeter a large amount of oatmeal was consumed, and the college had many plumbing problems in the seventeenth century. In one instance, the drain under the kitchen flooded six nearby houses and the college had to pay for repairs. In the 1670s and 1680s Jesus College was evidently plagued with rats in the kitchen and the larder as payments were made for killing the rodents in these two rooms. Pembroke, in 1758, paid £1/0/0 for the rent of a dung hole for five years.

Most of the colleges made periodic contributions to the poor prisoners in the Bocardo. The Bocardo was originally the name of the main gate in the North Wall which spanned the street beside St. Michael's Church to which it was adjoined. After the need for fortifications no longer existed, the room above the gate where Cranmer had been incarcerated, was used as a prison by the mayor and bailiffs for debtors and petty criminals. It was demolished in 1771. It was not a pleasant place in which to pass one's days.

A description of the prison was given in a 1661 report by the gentlemen who had been appointed to inspect the rooms which belonged to the City as opposed to those belonging to the Keeper of Bocardo. They wrote:

> the freemen's ward over the gate; the window looking up to Carfax;
> the inner ward within that on the north side;
> the women's ward with a little room within it on the west side of the prison;
> a little ward under the freemen's ward where the women beg;
> another ward where the men begge;

2

the Condemned Room under the women's ward;
the dungeon under that;
a vate and house of office under that.[2]

Vate probably refers to a cistern. Until about 1310 male and female prisoners shared the same room.[3]

The freemen's ward over the gate is where a freeman imprisoned for debt was lodged and where he could continue to work at his trade. It was only these freemen prisoners who had the right to hang out the bag. This was a bag which they lowered down to the street through the window facing Carfax for alms with the cry, "Pity the poor Bocardo birds."[4]

Felons and even those who were imprisoned for misdemeanors were dealt with harshly. In the early fourteenth century the keeper of the Bocardo was accused of beating his inmates. Even as late as 1754 there were stocks, collars, fettering irons, shackles, handcuffs and thumbscrews.[5] It was a place to be avoided, yet it took little provocation to become a prisoner there.

All Souls seems to have been the most generous benefactor to all sorts of causes. Besides contributions to the prisoners in the Bocardo, a poor woman with a sore breast, a distracted gentlewoman, disabled seaman, a cashiered lieutenant, a mad woman, and poor people of various nationalities including Arabian, Dutch, Welsh and Irish, all benefitted from the college's charity. The inhabitants of Warwick received £20, and payments were made to many individuals who suffered as a result of fires.

In December 1713 All Souls paid one Richard Warwick 14s. for killing the boar, and there were many entries over the years for boars. Large disbursements were made to the chandlers and brewers, which must have been true at all the colleges. As the eighteenth century approached, the accounts at Christ Church became increasingly concerned with candles and suppers.

It is from these accounts, however, that a picture emerges of the popularity, and therefore, presumed skill of certain goldsmiths. At the same time, however, it is not always possible to ascertain if the goldsmith is fulfilling specific orders as a working goldsmith or as a retailer. The evidence points to the fact that he was both. It appears to have been common

[2]OCA, 1626–1665, 286.
[3]Mary Jessup, *A History of Oxfordshire* (1975), 99.
[4]OCA, 1666–1701, xxxiii.
[5]Jessup, *op. cit.,* 99–100.

3

practice for articles of London workmanship to be sent up to Oxford to be engraved with armorials and/or inscriptions by local goldsmiths. As most of the plate acquired by the colleges consisted of gifts from old members, there was considerable such engraving to be done. As pieces became battered or worn out or were of a style which had fallen from favour, they were refashioned locally and engraved with the original donor's arms and notation of his gift although the new object may not have borne the slightest resemblance to the original gift. Only the metal was the same and possibly not all of that.

In our own age we are accustomed to handling old silver almost with reverence even when it is put to everyday use. It, therefore, makes it difficult to understand how objects fashioned of the precious metal could become so damaged. College servants probably did not exercise any particular care, perhaps for instance, grasping the handles of several tankards in one fist and clanking them together as they were carried from Hall. Much of the work of the Oxford goldsmiths consisted of mending the college plate, a term which implies soldering or patching. Beating and hammering were apparently employed to remove "bruises," otherwise known as dents.

Silver tarnishes and the means of cleaning it left a lot to be desired. There are frequent references to boiling, burnishing and planishing, but more damaging was the use of sand and bran for "scouring" it. The word "scouring" cannot be taken too literally as it was also used in reference to cleaning cloth; nevertheless, sand and bran could not have had a very salutary effect. Brushes were also used.

It is unfortunate that so very few of the objects the Oxford goldsmiths created have survived. Some of them must have been quite spectacular, especially the earlier ones. Much of this destruction was due to the Civil War when the Royalist Oxford colleges responded to the plea of Charles I to send their plate to the Mint in New Inn Hall Street. The nineteenth century witnessed the heavy hand of the Victorians with their passion for refashioning, especially anything having a plain unadorned surface.

The Beginnings

Oxford, like other cities in England has had its ups and downs. In the twelfth century when goldsmiths first begin to appear in the records, Oxford was a flourishing city with the burgesses having some of the same privileges that only London and Winchester had. The growing prosperity was due largely to the market and the variety of trades practiced in the town.

With the coming of the students and the beginnings of the University, Oxford polarized into two camps: Town and Gown, resulting in frequent riots, and with every riot the University nibbled away more of the town's privileges. The climate of the Thames Valley, and especially of Oxford, was damp (it still is) and this often led to sickness. There were also periodic hard winters which added to the suffering of the populace. The Black Death played havoc with the inhabitants, and even in the last quarter of the sixteenth century and the first quarter of the seventeenth it was a very unwholesome place. Some houses and parts of colleges were built on graveyards, streets were filled with dung and garbage leading to contamination of food and water. In all fairness, however, Oxford was probably no worse than other cities of the time. Good hygiene was yet to be discovered.

Finally, though, by the mid-sixteenth century prosperity returned and the number of tradesmen grew. A survey of the Hanaster Books between 1590 and 1640 provides a good picture of the trades which were necessary to supply the City and the University with important commodities. There were many cordwainers (shoemakers), tailors, mercers, quite a few woollen drapers, haberdashers, many butchers, cutlers, a lesser number of glaziers and plumbers (trades which were connected), a number of musicians, fellmongers (dealers in sheepskins and other animal skins), several boatmen, watermen, one tobacco pipemaker, a great many whitebakers, quite a few plasterers, slatters, many freemasons, one bricklayer, many vintners, very few gardeners, a few fullers, a few wheelwrights, very few falconers, and a few more pewterers than goldsmiths.

Fairs were held in Oxford probably as early as the eleventh century, and over the years they were the cause of squabbles and riots between

5

Town and Gown. There was a slow decline in popularity and thus profits, and by 1675 there were no fairs being held in Oxford. Goldsmiths were among the stall-holders in the late sixteenth century,[1] but there is no evidence that the wardens of the London Goldsmiths' Company ever made a search at the Oxford fairs as they were wont to do in other towns.

The earliest goldsmith found in Oxford records was Radulfo Aurifaber who held lands in St. Mary's parish of the fee of the Abbot of Oseney in 1180, but he may not have been living in the parish.[2] In 1215 goldsmiths were holding property in the center of Oxford. In that year Gauf Aurifaber granted to Walter, his eldest son, three messuages in the High Street. Walter died sometime before 1300, then from 1317 to 1324, his son, John Aurifaber, held the leases which had finally passed from the family by 1360. No. 132 High Street, next to the Chequers, was held from 1281 to 1340 by William Wyth, goldsmith, although Thomas Aurifaber was there in 1290. Nicholas Aurifaber was at 130 High Street from 1285 to 1302. Various other goldsmiths held land in the Turl, the Cornmarket and Magdalen Street in the thirteenth and fourteenth centuries.[3]

On December 3, 1257, at Westminster a complaint was made by Margaret, widow of Walter Biset, that before the justices in the County of Oxford, she had demised to Walter le Orfevre of Oxford, all her right in the name of dower in the land which had belonged to her husband in the parish of St. Martin's, Oxford, for the sum of 16s. which was to be paid to her annually under certain conditions which she would retain. Walter the Goldsmith, however, "removed the house and whole vesture" of the land which caused her to be unable to make distraint for the arrears of the said rent.[4]

In the rent rolls in the Cartulary of Oseney Abbey, one Helena Aurifaber is living in All Saints parish in 1317. It is unknown, however, whether she was actually a working goldsmith or perhaps the widow of a goldsmith. She may have been Elena, the wife of Nicholas, a goldsmith frequently mentioned in Oriel College deeds.[5]

---

[1] VCH, Oxfordshire, IV (1979), 310–312.

[2] C. L. Shadwell and H. E. Salter, eds., Oriel College Records (1926), 471.

[3] Vide Salter, Survey of Oxford, I and II, ed. by W. A. Pantin and W. T. Mitchell (1960 and 1969).

[4] Cal. Patent Rolls, 1247–1258, 658.

[5] Shadwell and Salter, op. cit., 376.

Robert le Goldsmith was a participant in the affray between Town and Gown which began on St. Scholastica's Day, February 10, 1354/5 in the Swyndlestock Tavern at Carfax.[6] The murderous mayhem which continued for three or four days began when some University clerks criticized the quality of the wine the vintner served them, and after a heated exchange of words, the clerks threw the wine and its vessel at the vintner's head. As a result the Town did penance until 1825.

The Poll Tax of 1380 records six goldsmiths in the Oxford population. They were Robert Dalham whose wife was Juliana, John Englisshe whose wife was Anastacia, John Iryssh who apparently did not have a wife, John Rammesbury whose wife was Agnete, William Steymour whose wife was Emma, and John Stokes whose wife was Isabella. Two of them were in the parish of Holywell. Johanne (John) Goldsmyth and his concubine Juliana, according to a fourteenth century lay subsidy, were residing in the parish of St. Mary the Virgin.[7] In the last years of the fourteenth century the constables were required to make a list of all labourers in their bailiwicks. Named were Carolus Goldsmyth aurifaber and Iohannes Goldsmythe aurifabrum.[8]

In the fifteenth century surnames other than Goldsmith or the Latin or Norman-French equivalent began to appear more frequently in deeds. In 20 Henry VI William Huchons, alias William Goldsmythe, granted a messuage and six shops in St. Ebbe's to a London mercer and his wife, as well as three messuages with solars and gardens near Exeter College. In 1441 Thomas Wylde, goldsmith, who may have been the same person as Thomas Goldsmith, held 62–64 Cornmarket.[9]

It is uncertain whether all of these goldsmiths actually lived and worked in Oxford or merely held property as a form of investment. A goldsmiths' quarter west of All Saints along the High and extending to St. Martin's, however, was recorded in 1259. It apparently reached farther east as well as there are some indications of goldsmiths working in the Turl.[10]

---

[6]J. E. Thorold Rogers, ed., *Oxford City Documents, 1268–1665* (1891), 245.
[7]*Ibid.*, 11 *et passim*.
[8]Salter, *Medieval Archives of the University of Oxford* (1921), II, 113–117.
[9]Salter, *Survey of Oxford*, I and II.
[10]*VCH, Oxfordshire*, IV, 27, citing *Oseney Cart.*, I, 436–437; Octavius Ogle, "The Oxford Market," in *Collectanea* (1890), II, 23–24.

Through various records other than those dealing with leases, it appears there was a considerable number of these artisans resident in the City. Some of them, at least, had an additional occupation as in the Assize of Ale at Michaelmas 1311, Nicholas Aurifaber and Thomas Aurifaber were listed as brewing and selling beer or ale. From then until May 1350, other goldsmiths were also following this pursuit; namely, Edwardus le Goldsmyth, Robert le Goldsmyth, and Roger le Goldsmyth.[11]

Edward le Goldsmyth is met again when he appeared at an inquest for Henry de Stodley who was found dead in his house in St. Peter-le-Bailey on Thursday, September 28, 1346. Edward and others said under oath that de Stodley (or Stodleghe) on Wednesday had been sitting in his hall after dinner with a naked knife in his hand, then rose to go to his chamber, but when he entered the chamber he stumbled, being drunk, fell on his knife and cut his throat which resulted in his death. They priced the knife at fourpence.[12] Probably this was the Henry de Stodley who was Mayor in 1344–1345. Edward le Goldsmyth and the others who gave testimony must have been dining with de Stodley on Wednesday so one wonders why the body was not discovered until Thursday. His guests probably were also drunk and not very aware of events until recovering the following day.

A number of Oxford goldsmiths played a rôle in City government during the Middle Ages. Galfridus (Geoffrey) Aurifaber is mentioned in City records during the reigns of Richard I and John and is believed to be Galfridus Stockwell who served as Mayor circa 1230 and again in 1238. Walterus (Walter) Aurifaber, Ricardus (Richard) Aurifaber, and Galfridus Aurifaber were taking part in local government at the time of Henry III. Galfridus was again mentioned during the reign of Edward I, as was Nicholas Aurifaber.

Beginning in 1239, the records show what specific rôle the goldsmiths were playing in governing the City. In that year the Mayor was Galfridus de Stockwell whose father was Richard, and in 1246, Nicholas de Stockwell, a brother of Galfridus, was Mayor. In that same year Galfridus Aurifaber, son of Galfridus was *praepositi*, which translates "commander" and may be taken to mean "alderman." In 1253 he was again mentioned, and then as bailiff in 1260, with his career in local government apparently ending in 1274. The last mention of Nicholas was in 1289 when he was Mayor.

In 1275 one Jeffry the goldsmith was mentioned, and in 1299, one John de orfeur appeared in the records. This may have been the Johannes

---

[11]Salter, *Medieval Archives of the University of Oxford*, 186 *et passim*.
[12]Salter, ed., *Records of Medieval Oxford. Coroners' Inquests, etc.* (1921), 39.

le orfeure who represented Oxford in a number of Parliaments between 1301 and 1322; and, in 1425/6, Thomas Goldsmythe of Oxford was in the Parliament that met at Leicester. More than a century passed before another goldsmith was active in the affairs of the City when, in 1416, William Huchons was bailiff. Nearly another century passed before another member of the craft is found in a city office when Roger Goldsmyth, alias Nywton (Newnton) was bailiff in 1510.[13] It was not a happy choice. In September 1511, he and the other bailiff, Nicholas Syers (Syre or Cere), butcher, were suspended by the University from entering church, followed by excommunication for contumacy in refusing to answer the summons of William Fauntleroy, commissary [vice-chancellor].[14]

Newnton's name had appeared several times in the Register of the Chancellor's Court. In 1498 he was an arbitrator in a dispute for which he received payment. February 23, 1502, William Arculez, goldsmith, was surety that John Tilston, goldsmith, who had been imprisoned for breach of the peace at the request of Roger Newton [sic], would behave well towards William Pery, keeper of the Bocardo, if his chains were removed. May 10 it was recorded that a final concord was made about the middle of Lent between John Tilston and Roger and Alice Newnton at the request of Tilston who presumably was adequately contrite. August 25, 1503, Alice Newnton, wife of Roger Newnton of the parish of St. Martin, swore that she was not a party to the theft of a piece of silver by her young servant from the house of Henry Cromp, publican. Five women swore that they believed she was telling the truth. James Tezsen, a Salisbury mercer, on May 8, 1504, declared he would not sue Roger Newynton, who is described as a privileged goldsmith, or Alice his wife, in another court. Unfortunately, there are no other details of this event or of what led up to it. Newnton's name appears as a surety April 18, 1505, that John Shoner, husbandman of Kidlington, would appear whenever he was required to do so before the Nativity of St. John the Baptist.[15]

George Strele was another goldsmith who made frequent appearances in the Chancellor's Court. He is first mentioned 13 September 1500 when John Jonson, bedel, had a silver crossfoot weighing 11½ ounces which

---

[13]Anthony Wood, *Survey of the Antiquities of the City of Oxford* [composed 1661–6], ed. by Andrew Clark (1899), III, 5 *et passim*.

[14]Turner, *Selections from the Records of the City of Oxford, 1509–1583*, 1; 1–2fn. *Univ. Reg.*, f.148.

[15]W. T. Mitchell, ed., *Registrum Cancellarii, 1498–1506* (1980), 31 *et passim*.

belonged to Strele. At the instigation of Jonson it was valued by Jonson and Christopher Coke, stationer, at 34s. 6d. Strele's troubles with the authorities began 28 October 1502 when he failed to indemnify Frederick Egmont, a London bookseller, and was imprisoned until he paid the £10 due Egmont. Before the year was out he was involved in a confusing case brought by Christopher Middleton, proctor of the Court of Arches, London, and was declared contumacious for his failure to appear.

It is unclear exactly what the charges against Strele were, but the case dragged on until May 1503 when "Middleton proved before the commissary and Hugh Peyntwyn, archdeacon of Canterbury, on 30 March at his house in London by the testimony of Dr. Battmanson, LL.D. and John Bell, clerk of the court, that his wife had deposited with George Strele, goldsmith, a golden rosary, a turquoise and an emerald." Strele promised to visit Middleton in London a fortnight after Easter under penalty of 20 marks. The emerald was valued at £3/0/0. Strele stated that Middleton owed him; i.e., 20s. for a rose bottle of silver, 13s. 4d. for making a pair of beads of gold, and 2s. for making a ring.

At the same time this case was dragging on, Lincoln College brought a case before the court to collect 20s. from Strele for the bond as surety for William Haus who was involved in a dispute with the college over unpaid rent. It appears that Strele tried unsuccessfully to claim it was not his signature on the bond. In 1504, however, he was entrusted to examine the contents of a casket of jewels "in the presence of good men and seal it." The jewels had been deposited with Dr. Thornton to be delivered to Agnes Harrys, widow, for whose indemnity they were pledged.[16]

Henry Spankoe, goldsmith, was a surety for John Fustynge, carver, February 6, 1501,[17] the only mention made of him. James Goldsmyth (Iacobus Vanoxferd) twice was a surety for George Strele during his court proceedings.[18] His name seems to indicate that he may have been Dutch. Dr. Slyngebryge in August of 1502 delivered a silver salt-cellar to James Goldsmyth for another to be made out of it, but its cover and middle part got into the hands of Severinus, servant of Frederick de Egmond, that London bookseller, who pawned them for 8s.[19] January 15, 1509/10, William Hercles, goldsmith, was mentioned in a case in the Chancellor's Court regarding the pawning of 67 oz. of silver consisting of four cups,

[16]*Ibid.*, 89 *et passim.*
[17]*Ibid.*, 92.
[18]*Ibid.*, 141; 145.
[19]*Ibid.*, 132.

twelve spoons, and one salt-cellar as well as three rings.[20] This lot of Oxford goldsmiths seemed prone to nefarious dealings.

In order to put a stop to the forging of money on the Continent which flowed into England, the importation of any coined money was prohibited by King and Parliament at Westminster March 13, 1327. Only fine silver in plate could be imported, and gold and silver, goldsmiths' work, or silver in plate could be sold only at the King's Exchange or openly in the Goldsmiths' quarter for use and not for resale. Exportation was forbidden. The Goldsmiths were to elect some of the members of the Company who were given the power to search out and punish offenders. These same ordinances were to apply to every city and town in England where goldsmiths were working. It was further ordained that one or two goldsmiths from each of these places should go to London "to obtain from the mistery their fixed touch of gold and also their stamp of a puncion with the leopard's head."[21]

On October 14, 1328, at Marlborough a mandate was issued to the mayor and bailiffs of Oxford to cause those ordinances to be observed in Oxford. Thomas de Berkyng, Henry de la More, Robert de Shordich, and Hugh le FitzRogier, goldsmiths and wardens of the London Company, appointed Edward de Wircestr' (Worcester), goldsmith of Oxford to enforce the ordinances.[22]

It seems that the craft languished in the fourteenth and fifteenth centuries. The Black Death may have been partly responsible for the apparent dearth of goldsmiths in the mid-fourteenth century. Wills proved and enrolled in the Court of Husting, London, show that seventeen members of the London Goldsmiths' Company died in the terrible years of 1348 and 1349. On the other hand Salter makes the observation that "it is incidentally stated in 1348 that the mercers, goldsmiths, and others had gilds."[23] It is doubtful, though, how influential any of the guilds were since they could not make any ordinances without the approval of the Mayor and burgesses.[24] The next mention of a goldsmiths' guild was in 1524 and 1525 when the guild had a Mass in All Saints Church on

[20]University Archives, Calendar Chancellor's Court Register F Reversed, 1506–1515, f.78r. This is probably the same man as William Arculez and William Arcles, names appearing in the Chancellor's Court in 1502.

[21]*Cal. Patent Rolls, 1327–1330*, 42–43.

[22]*Ibid.*, 323.

[23]Salter, *Medieval Oxford* (1936), 63

.[24]*Ibid.*, 64.

Whitsunday in those two years.[25] The next definite mention of a gold-smith is in 1529/30 when John Honchert was granted his freedom.[26]

In the first half of the sixteenth century the names of goldsmiths appear with greater frequency. Owen Draper gained his freedom in 1541/2,[27] and William Pynfold in 1546/7.[28] On November 2, 1548, Francis Gore, son of Richard Gore of Abingdon, Berkshire, was apprenticed to Alias Allen the Elder of the City of Oxford, goldsmith.[29] Charles Dynmock, goldsmith, apprentice of Alan Preston, was made a freeman in 1552/3,[30] and Dionisius Colman likewise in 1574/5.[31] January 23, 1575/6, Colman took an apprentice, Thomas Vaughan, son of Moris Vaughan of the City of Oxford, mercer.[32] With the exception of Alan Preston and William Pynfold, little more is known of these master goldsmiths or their apprentices.

Alan Preston makes three brief appearances in the Chancellor's Court Register. Leonard Warden had borrowed a horse and bridle from him and failed to return it at the stipulated time, and the horse was found to be injured. Preston sued him 10 January 1531/2 for about 33s. 4d., but the court decided that 29s. 8d. was sufficient recompense for Preston.[33]

Another time he was not as fortunate. April 22, 1531, the court decided that Alan Preston, goldsmith, who had refused to appear before the proctor, John Pollard, in connection with a breach of the peace, was to answer to the proctor when required on pain of imprisonment.[34] It is not known if he complied with the order. Noted in the Register February 20, 1532/3 are details of silver being deposited by various members of the University in the several Chests. Some spoons deposited in the Ruthbery Chest by Richard Dowtie and Antony Tallboushe and redeemed by Edmund Campion, S.T.B. were said by Alan Preston, goldsmith, to have been made by him for Henry Hawworth.[35]

[25]*Ibid.*, 63.
[26]Turner, *op. cit.*, 93.
[27]*Ibid.*, 167.
[28]*Ibid.*, 189.
[29]Hanaster Book, 1514–1591, A.5.3.
[30]Turner, *op. cit.*, 216.
[31]*Ibid.*, 375.
[32]Hanaster Book, 1514–1591, A.5.3.
[33]Calendar Chancellor's Court Register EEE, 1527–1545; 1557, Part I, 1527–1535, f.197r.
[34]*Ibid.*, f.183v.
[35]*Ibid.*, f.204r. Campion is now known as St. Edmund Campion, S. J.

It is William Pynfold (spelled variously, Pynfold, Pynfolde, Pynnefolde), though, who is the really colourful character. He seems to have been one of those people who could not stay out of trouble no matter where he was. There is nothing known about his life before he gained his freedom in Oxford in 1546/7 except that his daughter Joan was baptized at St. Petrock's, Exeter, in 1546. He was in Oxford, however, in 1548/9 when on March 2 a complaint was made in the Chancellor's Court by John Herynge who said he handed to Pynfold, goldsmith, an angelot of old gold and an equal amount of gold fragments with a value of 27 staterae. Pynfold claimed that he delivered "a counterpece of the golde to Herynge and was told by the judge to deliver the ring "eight days ago." He was in trouble again 27 April when he failed to appear and was declared contumacious by James Edmundes, chief bedel of arts, acting as proxy for John Pollar, archdeacon of Barnstaple, who had made the request. He was to be fined and cited again.[36]

Pynfold was either slow in completing work with which he was entrusted or he deliberately attempted to purloin some of the material given to him for the project at hand. This again brought him to the attention of the authorities, and on July 17, John Kenall claimed that Richard Ramsey had deposited a crown of good gold, part of a ring of fine gold weighing half a crown and a jacinth (an orange-colour gem stone) worth 40s. He was to make a ring from these materials or else return them. Pynfold did not get around to making the ring, as on 20 July it was noted that he had returned to Ramsey a crown of good gold and a piece of the old angelot, and he was to come to an understanding with Ramsey about the jacinth within a week.[37] The matter appears to have been settled amicably. Less than a year later, though, Pynfold was in trouble again. In the Chancellor's Court on 5 April 1549 he was duly cited, and since he had not appeared, was ordered to be imprisoned.[38] No details are given of what the offense might have been which resulted in his incarceration or of how long he languished in prison.

The University authorities must have been greatly relieved when he left Oxford and returned to Exeter where he was admitted to the freedom of the City upon payment of £1/6/8 sometime between April and Michaelmas 1557. During those intervening eight years his whereabouts are

---

[36]Calendar Chancellor's Court Register GG Hyp/a/5, 1545–1555, f.28r.
[37]*Ibid.*, f.29v.
[38]*Ibid.*, f.34r.

unknown. It is unlikely that he was in prison that long. The archdeacon of Barnstaple seemed aware of his reputation, so his return to Devon could not have been welcomed.

In Exeter he made known his contentious views regarding the City's government and method of electing a mayor. This was duly reported in the Chamber March 1, 1559/60. The following year he was in more serious trouble. On December 17, 1561, he was summoned to appear before the Mayor on a variety of charges. He was accused of using "typlinge and sellinge of ale and beare and keeping typling in his house" and that he kept "an Innehouse without any signe hanginge at his Doore." It was also asserted that he had harboured suspicious persons and spoke threats to the Stewards of the City. The result of Pynfold's misbehaviour was prison where he was to remain without bail until he provided sufficient evidence of good behaviour in the future.[39] It is a bit difficult to comprehend how one could accomplish that while in prison.

It is not known how long this prison stay was, but by 8 November 1564 he was in even deeper trouble. That day a presentation was made by the City Constable to the Mayor and Stewards that William Pynnefold had committed fornication and adultery with one Jane Harton in a ditch of a close held by Pynfold outside Eastgate. The first time was in the week after Easter, and other times followed but the Constables were unsure of the number. They claimed, too, that with his own hands he gave her 16d. and also sent a like amount to her by one Willmot Toker. Pynfold denied the sordid affair and a jury acquitted him.[40] With this he disappears from the records.

Next to nothing is known about the work done by these earliest Oxford goldsmiths. Between 1480 and 1481 a payment of 2s. 3d. was made for mending a chalice used in the Lady Chapel of St. Michael-at-the-North Gate. An additional charge was made for an ounce of silver "that was put to the chalys," but the goldsmith's name was not recorded.[41] In 1507/8 William Goldsmyth was paid 12d. by Magdalen College for mending the great Crucifix standing above the altar and for mending the pax.[42] In the same year he also did work for Oriel College.[43] On May 31

[39]Exeter Chamber Act Book IV, 14.

[40]*Ibid.*, 266–267. I am indebted to Timothy Kent for the information regarding Pynfold's exploits in Exeter.

[41]Salter, The Churchwardens' Accounts of St. Michael's Church, Oxford, 1404–1562, in *Transactions of the Oxfordshire Archaeological Society*, #78 (1933), 110.

[42]Bloxam, *A Register of St. Mary Magdalen College* (1857), II, 263.

[43]Oriel College Treasurer's Accounts, ETC B2.

and again on July 4, 1508, he served as an arbitrator in the Chancellor's Court.[44]

St. Michael-at-the-North Gate in 1512–1513 paid William Goldsmyth 3s. 10d. for the mending of a chalice belonging to the church. There are several early mentions in the parish accounts of mending chalices, the altar cruets, and the cross. During the year between March 12, 1536/7 and March 12, 1537/8, the churchwardens apparently gave up on the mending and sold a broken chalice for 34s. 4d., another chalice for £3/9/8, and two cruets for 6s. 8d. No goldsmith is named in any of these transactions. During the same period of 1549/50–1550/1, the parish bought a book of the new service for 4s. 2d., but there is no mention of refashioning the chalice into a Communion cup.[45] One wonders how altar plate could be so misused to become so broken.

These early goldsmiths surely did not rely solely on the University, the colleges, and the churches for employment. There was a considerable amount of wealth among the inhabitants of Oxford and wills which survive attest to this. For instance, Thomas Bloxham, whose Prerogative Court of Canterbury will is dated 21 April 1473, left an array of plate. This priest and former fellow of Merton College, directed that he was to be buried in the church of St. Frideswide, Oxford. He left to John Page, one of his executors, one pair of silver salts, "my best piece covered with gilt," and twelve silver spoons. Merton was to receive one covered salt and another, not covered. He ordered his executors to have new-made a silver-gilt cover for the silver cup of the Prior and Convent of St. Frideswide with the greatest image of that virgin which could be placed on the top of the cover. To John Wyllys, Bloxham's nephew, he willed a silver covered cup which had been bought from Master Richard Luke. Merton, besides books to be chained in the library, was to receive three silver pots, one of which was gilt. Small uncovered silver pieces were to be distributed to the cleric's relatives according to their degree of kinship.[46]

More than a century later, the July 26, 1585 will of Roger Hewett, Alderman, who lived in the parish of St. Mary Magdalen, then described as being in the suburbs of Oxford, also left a considerable amount of plate. Included were double-gilt salts, goblets and cups, four "lyon spoones of silver, six silver spoones with mayden heades, my greate silver spoone

---

[44]Calendar Chancellor's Court Register F Reversed, 1506–1515, f.61v.

[45]Salter, *Transactions*, 190 *et passim*.

[46]P.R.O., P.C.C. Will of Thomas Bloxham [9 Wattys].

double gilte, six Appostell spoones of silver, and my lesser stone cup with silver."[47] It is quite possible that at least some of the silver mentioned in these wills was locally made.

In 1240 with the founding of the first loan chest, the University began to accumulate books, manuscripts, plate and jewels, and by 1500 the plate and jewellery dominated. Then in 1544/5 there occurred the Great Robbery. At about 9 o'clock in the evening of 21 February Robert Rounce, formerly a yeoman of High Wyckham, Bucks., and an Oxford scholar, and John Stanshaw, formerly of Reading, Berkshire, but of Oxford, gentleman, armed themselves with an iron bar, a hammer, and a pair of pincers and broke into the University Church of St. Mary the Virgin. Then they slipped into the chapel of John Langland, Chancellor of the University, which was known as the University Nether Chapel and where the Chest of the Five Keys was kept. Equipped as they were, there was no need for the five keys.

The two thieves made off with, among other things, flat silver pieces, two silver cups, three silver-gilt chalices, one silver salt-cellar, forty-two silver spoons, silver and gold weighing forty ounces, girdles called harness girdles, a gold bowl, twenty-two gold rings and a gold spoon valued at a hundred pounds. The harness girdles were possibly the bands from mazers.

Not satisfied with this loot, they returned eleven days later at about the same hour and broke into the High Congregation House. This time they made off with a silver-gilt Crucifix and a standing silver-gilt Crucifix, a silver-gilt girdle called the Duke Humfrey's girdle, and two silver-gilt candelabra, two phials called cruets, a silver thurible and a silver-gilt incense boat to the value of £100/10/4.

Dr. Leonard Hutcheson, Master of University College, had an agreement with Mr. Gounter, goldsmith, who seemed to be the University's goldsmith. Gounter was apparently entrusted with picking up the broken pieces of plate left behind by the thieves. He even swept up 3 ⅛ ounces of precious metal dust. For all of it he paid 12s. at the rate of 3s. 10d. per ounce—small compensation considering the value of what was stolen. Plate and jewels were cash to the University, and suddenly it was realized that bills could not be paid.[48]

---

[47]P.R.O., P.C.C. Will of Roger Hewett [16 Spencer].
[48]Pantin and Mitchell, eds., *The Register of Congregation, 1448–1463* (1972). 419–429.

The reason it would seem likely that Mr. Gounter was the University's goldsmith (the same craftsman tended to be used for a lifetime) is that Hutcheson had other dealings with him. Whenever the coffers were devoid of actual cash and payments needed to be made, Dr. Hutcheson had the authority to sell some of the plate or jewellery from the loan chests. "Urgent causes" seem to have occurred with considerable frequency. Most of the sales apparently were made up of broken plate. For example, Hutcheson received from Mr. Smythe, proctor, two pieces of a drinking pot, thirteen spoons weighing a total of forty-five ounces, and a chalice and paten which seem to have been whole. Smythe also brought in three rings and a gold buckle weighing 1 ½ ounces.

Five lots including those described totalled 300 ounces, four score nine and a half, all sold to Mr. Gounter (or Gownter). There were other sales to him and one to "Brygwater" of two little pieces weighing seventeen ounces for which 3s. 8d. per ounce was received making a total of £3/2/4.[49] Who Brygwater might have been is a mystery. His name never appears again in any records. Mr. Gownter refers to Richard Gounter, a bailiff of Oxford whose house was in the parish of St. Peter-le-Bailey. In 1529, however, he had been living in St. Martin's parish when he was an arbitrator in the Chancellor's Court.[50] He was the subject of proceedings to maintain his good name October 8, 1531, having been accused by some that his servant, William Ackrygge had not died in the pestilence, but rather from some punishment that Gounter had given him.[51] Richard Gunter [sic], alderman, took the oath in 1547 and 1548 to observe the privileges of the University.[52]

It seems highly unlikely that these deals would have been made with a London goldsmith and none of that name appears in lists of members of the London Company. On the other hand, there is no evidence that Gownter was a working goldsmith. His name does not appear in the Hanaster Books, but he does make frequent appearances in the Chancellor's Court Registers. On December 17, 1527, Richard Gownter and Alice Mason, widow, submitted their dispute about a bowl for which

---

[49]R. H. Hill, "The University Plate in the Sixteenth Century," *Bodleian Quarterly Record*, IV (1924, no. 421), 141–142. Gownter is referred to here as a goldsmith, but there is no proof that he was.

[50]Calendar Chancellor's Court Register EEE. 1527–1545; 1557, Part I, 1527–1535.

[51]Turner, *op. cit.,* 104.

[52]Andrew Clark, *Reg. of the Univ. of Oxford*, II, part I, introduction (1887), 296–297.

Alice was said to be in debt to Gownter, to the arbitration of Michael Hethe and William Fryar, aldermen.[53] Could this bowl have been silver?

From then until his death in 1553, he was involved in providing lodging and provisions for students and in brewing. After his death, his widow, who was his executrix, promised to return the equivalent of some timber lent to her late husband by Oriel and to supply the college with some lime. Richard Gownter seems to have been simply an entrepreneur who was frequently at odds with the University authorities which resulted in his appearances in the Chancellor's Court, and at times being declared contumacious for not appearing. At one point he went into hiding and was fined 7s., and finally was threatened with excommunication.[54]

The Chancellor wrote on July 7, 1566, "The Queen is coming to Oxford; make preparations for her reception." Two days later it was decided that the expenses of her visit should be paid by the "Custodes clavium" (keeper of the keys?).[55] Vivian Green of Lincoln College wrote in *The Illustrated History of Oxford University* (1993) that the three University staves which are now in the Ashmolean Museum were purchased for the Queen's visit. This hardly seems plausible since she arrived in August making for a very short time for any goldsmith to produce three staves. They were made in 1566 as shown by the accounts of the Vice-Chancellor, Dr. John Kennall. The University paid £59/6/8 for them,[56] but it is most unfortunate that the name of the goldsmith is not stated.

A close examination of the staves leads to the conclusion that they were locally made as the work appears to be too crude to have been produced in a London workshop. If, in fact, they were ordered after notice of the Queen's impending visit was received, it seems imperative that a local goldsmith be employed. The only known possibility is Thomas Gowre (or Gower) who was admitted to the freedom of the City in 1565/6,[57] and was known to be doing business with the University in 1569.[58]

Little more than a year after the staves were made the bedels were evidently complaining that they were too heavy as on 9 December 1567, a

---

[53]Calendar Chancellor's Court Register EEE, 1527–1545; 1557, Part I, 1527–1535, f.51r.

[54]*Vide* above Calendar; Part II, 1536–1545, 1557, and Calendar Register GG Hyp/A/5, 1545–1555, various entries.

[55]Clark, *op. cit.*, 234.

[56]University Archives, WPB/21/4, p. 64.

[57]Turner, *op. cit.*, 315.

[58]Clark, *op. cit.*, 338–339.

committee was appointed to consider the weight of the staves before the beginning of next Term.[59] This is not surprising as although the silver is not of an unduly thick guage and is wrapped around a wooden core, the heads are large fluted iron cones. Perhaps the staves were designed to be more than ceremonial accouterments. The heads could be useful for coshing a malefactor. The sixteenth century like the one before it could not be labeled an age of gentility.

[59]Ibid., 260.

Thomas Gower

The earliest Oxford goldsmith about whom more is known is Thomas Gower [or Gowre]. The first mention of him is in 1565/6 when he was admitted to the freedom of the City, then on September 29, 1570, he became a member of the Common Council.[1] Nothing is known of his family, nor of his birth, and there is no record of his apprenticeship.

April 3, 1567 Gower was licensed by the University to sell parchment. In 1569, 1576, 1587, and 1594 he is listed as a citizen and tradesman having contact with the University.[2] On 27 April 1587 he was licensed to sell ale as a tavern-keeper. The University issued the license and the licensee was required to give sureties that gambling, known as unlawful games, and the eating of meat on fasting days would not be permitted on the premises. Gower was said to be of Holywell parish.[3]

July 31, 1567 Edmund Pooley, son of Richard Pooley of Melling in the County of Lancaster, yeoman, was apprenticed to Thomas Gower of the City of Oxford, goldsmith, for a term of eight years. The parties entered into an unusual and puzzling arrangement with William Pooley of the City of Oxford, tailor, (presumably a relative) by which Thomas Gower was to "have hold occupy receave and enjoye all Lands Tenements, rents . . . all other herediments whatsoever" that Edmund Pooley would have in Lancashire after the death of his mother, Katherin, during the eight year term of his apprenticeship, provided that his mother died before the end of the term and that Edmund lived to complete his apprenticeship, then Thomas Gower could "lawfully distrain upon all such lands and for all rents due and the arrearages." The agreement was signed on August 26, 1567,[4] and was probably in lieu of the usual payment made by an ap-

[1]Turner, *Selections from the Records of the City of Oxford,* 315; 333.
[2]Clark, *Reg. of the Univ. of Oxford,* II, Part I Introduction, 338.
[3]*Ibid.,* 322–326.
[4]Hanaster Book, 1514–1591, A.5.3.

prentice or his family to the master. Presumably Edmund Pooley, provided he completed his apprenticeship, returned to Lancashire to practice his craft, as he does not appear further in Oxford records.

February 11, 1575/6 Thomas Gower took another apprentice, William Wright, son of Robert Wright of the City of Oxford, tailor.[5] Wright was destined to be the founder of a dynasty of goldsmiths and City Fathers. In that same year, Gower was one of the fifty-eight burgesses summoned to swear to observe the privileges of the University.[6] Gower had more than one occupation; in fact several, as has been noted. When he took an apprentice, Julius Periman, son of William Periman of London, musician, deceased, November 7, 1579, he was described as goldsmith and woollen draper.[7] There is no indication of which trade Periman was to learn, and there is no further record of him.

In 1582 Thomas Gower was occupying a garden "outside the town, between the road north, and the Town Wall South." The property was partly in the parish of St. Michael and partly in the parish of St. Mary Magdalen. March 28, 1586, he was to have the lease of a cellar which had recently been dug under the street by his house and "to have his post and his bulk standing out as now." The lease from Oriel College was for thirty years at a rent of 5s.[8] October 25, 1588 Mr. Gower was to have a lease of his cellar and certain windows set out for 40 years, rent 5s.[9] This may refer to the same property. In 1597 there is reference made to the tenement previously leased by the college to Thomas Gower, goldsmith, at No. 1, St. Aldate's.[10]

Oriel is the only college which records any work having been done by him. In 1586 he was paid 16s. for cleaning a salt and for repairing a cup.[11] Nothing more is known of him.

[5]*Ibid.*
[6]Clark, *op. cit.,* 303.
[7]Hanaster Book, 1514–1591, A.5.3.
[8]Salter, *Oxford City Properties* (1926), 250, 144–145.
[9]*OCA, 1583–1626,* 45.
[10]Salter, *op. cit.,* 144.
[11]Oriel College Treasurers' Accounts.

George Cary

George Cary [various spellings], son of Henry Carye of Sutton Montague, Somerset, husbandman, was apprenticed to William Wright of the City of Oxford, goldsmith, August 18, 1589.[1] Sutton Montague is apparently Sutton Montis, which was originally known as Sutton Montague. It is a small parish six miles southwest from Wincanton and seven or eight miles from Castle Cary[2] which was the place of origin of other goldsmithing Carys.

George Cary did not complete his apprenticeship in Oxford as in 1591, he was apprenticed for seven years to John Wilkins, citizen and goldsmith of London under the London Company. On November 10, 1598, he received his freedom.[3] This John Wilkins was probably the goldsmith Heal lists as being at Lombard Street in 1576, and who was buried in 1600.

Daniel Cary, a native of Castle Cary, Somerset, was apprenticed under the London Company and received his freedom in 1604, becoming a prolific spoonmaker. When he died in 1642, he left a bequest to the London Goldsmiths' Company which was used to make four beer bowls. The coat-of-arms used by Daniel Cary was engraved on the bowls. Timothy Kent surmises the arms had been purloined from the family of Cary, Viscounts Falkland with which there was no apparent connection.[4]

The link between George Cary and Daniel Cary has not been established and the parish registers of Sutton Montis are not extant prior to 1701. They certainly must have been of the same family. One is led to speculate, however, why George Cary first chose to go to Oxford rather than London for his apprenticeship. No other apprentice came from so far away with the exception of Edmund Pooley from Lancashire, the ap-

[1]Hanaster Book, 1514–1591, A.5.3.
[2]MS., Letter from Somerset Record Office, September 2, 1993.
[3]MS., Information from the Archives of Timothy Arthur Kent, November 1993.
[4]T. A. Kent, *London Silver Spoonmakers, 1500–1697* (1981), 26–27.

prentice of Thomas Gower. He, however, evidently had a relative living in Oxford, the tailor, William Pooley. This may have been so of George Cary as a Robert Cary was living in All Saints when his daughter was baptized 12 July 1576. Perhaps George and Daniel Cary were connected in some way to the Falklands, possibly through the younger sons of a cadet line. Sir Lawrence Tanfield's only child, Elizabeth, married Henry Cary, the first Viscount Falkland, in 1600, and they lived at Burford Priory, only eighteen miles from Oxford.

About the time that George Cary received his freedom he married Sarah, daughter of Edward Harford of a well-known Bristol family, and became established there being admitted a Burgess March 6, 1614/15. He had at least two sons during the approximately sixteen years of his marriage, his wife being buried at Christ Church, Bristol, September 2, 1614. His own date of death and burial is as yet unknown. A brother of George Cary, Edmond, was apprenticed to the important London goldsmith, John Middleton in 1608.[5]

[5]Archives of T. A. Kent. According to Heal, George Cary was in St. Mary Woolnoth from 1600 to 1610.

Thomas Crompton

Not a great deal is known about most of the goldsmiths who were apprenticed in Oxford before 1600. One about whom there are a few more facts is Thomas Crompton, variously spelled Crampton and Crumpton in the records. He was the son of a London grocer, Richard Crompton, deceased, and was apprenticed to William Wright of the City of Oxford, goldsmith, 5 June 1594.[1]

The first mention of his work was 24 October 1600 when Christ Church College paid him £8/8/0 for a salt weighing "30 ounces & a half & half a quarter at 5s. 6d. per ounce."[2] It must have been a magnificent piece of silver. November 15, 1609, the college paid him 5s. 11d. for the verplus of a cup given by Mr. Butler, Mr. Gardner and four others,[3] and in 1612 he engraved twelve spoons at a cost of 3s.[4] During the previous year he had made a standing cup with a ewer of silver and a gilt dish weighing nearly 30 ounces at 6s. 10d. per ounce. The cost was £10/4/0.[5] The only other mention of work being done by Crompton appears as a 10s. payment to him by University College at an unspecified date.[6] Hiscock surmises that the beautiful gilt steeple cup and cover belonging to Brasenose may be the work of Thomas Crompton. Bearing the London hallmarks for 1610 and a maker's mark TC, it may well have come from his hand, but with a lack of documentation it can be no more than plausible speculation.

Thomas Crompton's only apprentice was Thomas Busbye, son of John Busbye of the City of Oxford, cordwainer, who was enrolled 8 June

[1]Hanaster Book, 1590–1614, L.5.1.
[2]Christ Church College MS. xii.b.45.
[3]*Ibid.*, xii.b.54. Verplus probably refers to gilding [vermeil].
[4]*Ibid.*, xii.b.57.
[5]W. G. Hiscock, *A Christ Church Miscellany* (1946), 136.
[6]University College MSS. These accounts are very sketchy, so the date cannot be ascertained positively.

1621.[7] This was probably Thomas Busbie, son of John who was baptized 10 June 1604 at St. Peter-le-Bailey. His mother's name was probably Mary as 6 September 1609, John Busbye, son of John and Mary Busbey was baptized at St. Peter-le-Bailey. Thomas Busbye would have been seventeen years old at the time of his apprenticeship, a later age than usual. Nothing more is known of him.

Little is known of Crompton's private life. The first mention of him in the Council Acts is 15 December 1603 when it was noted:

> Richard Fly, hatter, to have £25 of Sir Thomas White's money which George Crompton, mercer, had, for the residue of the years that were granted to Crompton, finding sufficient sureties; if he fails to find them, then Thomas Crompton, goldsmith, to have it, finding sufficient sureties.[8]

George Crompton, who was from Staffordshire, and Thomas Crompton apparently were not related.

October 2, 1609, Thomas Crompton was elected to the Common Council, and by the next spring he had become a thorn in the side of the Council. On 18 May he and fourteen others were fined 4d. each for coming into the Council House wearing their cloaks, but without their gowns.[9] By September he was again in trouble with the Council for unseemly speech and on the 28th of that month:

> At a meeting of the most part of the thirteene in the Offyce, it is agreed and ordered that whereas it doth appeare unto them that Thomas Crompton, goldsmyth, a citizen of this Cyttie, hath at the last Counsell spoken and uttered against the whole howse certeine slanderous words, viz. in saying that the howse had done contrarie to their othes, and further said onto one of the same howse that he was forsworne in yielding to some thing there done by consent and so were all the rest; It is then ordered that the same Thomas Crompton shall at the next Counsaile before all the said howse there assembled confess and acknowledge that he had or did by speaking the words aforesaid abuse or injure the said companie or the more parte of them, consenting as before, and that he did the same ippon erroe, as he saith; which order if he doe not in manner and forme as before said, then to pay unto the use of the Cyttie fyve pownds.[10]

[7]Hanaster Book, 1613–1640, L.5.2.
[8]OCA, 1583–1626, 158.
[9]Ibid., 194, 296, 199–200.
[10]Ibid., 202–203.

In spite of his transgressions he continued to hold office for a number of years. From 1611 to 1616, he was chamberlain until 12 July 1616 for 50s. he was made a bailiff, a two-year post to which he was repeatedly named until 29 September 1625.[11] In 1626 his name was entered as bailiff, then crossed out with no explanation.[12] Crompton was one of the fifty-eight burgesses summoned to swear to observe the privileges of the University in 1614, 1615, 1617, 1619 and 1621.[13] His political career was over but he had managed to keep his peace after the early stormy years.

In the Churchwardens Accounts for St. Martin's parish his name appears as a vestryman for seven years between 1610 and 1624, and on the tax list of 1619, he paid 13s. 4d.[14] There is no record of his leasing property, but he obviously lived in the center of the city.

Very little is known about his family. His first born, Thomas, who came into the world sporting three teeth, was baptized at St. Martin's 6 October 1605. Living less than eight years, he was buried there 14 April 1613. Another son, John, was baptized 14 October 1610, and a daughter, Marye, 11 October 1612. His wife, whose Christian name is unknown, was buried at St. Martin's 26 August 1625, and on 15 December of the same year, their daughter, Eadith, followed her to the grave. No baptismal record has been found for her. Thomas Crompton then would have been about 46 years old.

A license was granted by the Bishop of London November 4, 1626 for the marriage of Thomas Crompton, Gentleman, of the City of Oxford, widower, age 47, and Joane Larchin of St. Michael, Queenhithe, London, widow, age 45, with the ceremony to be performed at St. Olave's, Silver Street, London. It is probable that he moved to London after his marriage, and thus the reason for his name being struck off as bailiff in 1626. This was the first mention of him as "gentleman," and there is no evidence that he continued to work as a goldsmith.

[11]*Ibid.*, 217 *et passim.*
[12]*OCA, 1626–1665,* 2.
[13]Clark, *Reg. of the Univ. of Oxford,* II, Part I Introduction, 308 *et passim.*
[14]Oxon. Archives, D. D. Par. Oxford St. Martin's a.1. (1540–1680).

Thomas Berry

Thomas Berry was born in the ancient wool town of Chipping Norton, Oxfordshire, where he was baptized in the parish church of St. Mary the Virgin 28 January 1594/5, the son of Richard Berry and Ane Treadwell who had been married in the same church 15 February 1589/90. Richard, son of Micahell Berrie, had been baptized there sometime between 22 January 1564/5 and 31 March 1565. Thomas had an older sister, Sara, baptized 8 July 1593. Their mother was buried 13 October 1598, and a few months later on 16 May 1599, Richard married again, this time to Ane Jordine. Their son, Richard, was baptized in February of 1599/1600.

In the apprenticeship record of Thomas Berry, his father is given as "mercer," but by the time he was buried 5 August 1626, he was listed in the parish register as "gentleman." Like other members of the Berry family, he evidently was a substantial citizen of Chipping Norton as when the town was incorporated as a free borough by Royal Charter in February 1606/7, Richard Berry was named as one of the first twelve burgesses.[1]

On 10 July 1609, Thomas Berry was apprenticed to Walter Wilkins of the City of Oxford, goldsmith, and 2 July 1618, he was admitted to the freedom of the City.[2] The earliest mention of any work being done by him is in 1623 when Exeter College paid him £4/0/0.[3] In the Buttery Accounts of Jesus College in 1636 is an entry "To Berry ye Goldsmith" for mending plates, 9s." From then until 1663 there were five subsequent payments made to "the Goldsmith" unnamed for mending and exchanging and changing plate with the largest sum being £5/8/0. It appears that once a certain goldsmith was employed he was named in the first entry and then was only "the Goldsmith" until a different goldsmith was employed by

[1]Eileen Meader, *The History of Chipping Norton,* 2nd ed. (1984), 47–48.
[2]Hanaster Books, 1590–1614, L.5.1.; 1613–1640, L.5.2.
[3]Exeter College, A.II.9 [1566–1639].

the college and the procedure was repeated. It is probable that these further entries referred to Berry.[4]

His principal work seems to have been done for New College which paid him £29/9/6 on 3 January 1649/50, under the heading "Plate sould [*sic*] to New College," thus marking a rather early attempt on the part of the college to replace the plate which had been contributed to Charles I to be melted into coinage at the Oxford Mint with which to pay his troops. This sum was the cost of one "greate salte weight 26 oz. & 3 qurts 8 dwt. two trencher salts wt. 4 oz. halfe & halfe qurt one tankerd wt. 27 oz. halfe one porringer wt. 8 oz. 3 qurts less 1 dwt. one dozen of spoones wt. 21 oz. halfe less 3 dwt. For engraving the Coll: armes upon all ye plate and spoones paid for the carriage of the salte and tankerd to and from London."[5]

This last phrase "paid for the carriage of the salte and tankerd to and from London" is significant. It proves that all this plate was actually made by Thomas Berry, but even more important it indicates that these two large pieces were sent to Goldsmiths' Hall for assay and marking. If Berry had registered his mark in London, there would be no record of it surviving as the Goldsmiths' Company are not known to have kept any such records before 1697, and the relevant pieces of plate no longer exist at New College. However, Jackson and Pickford illustrate four unascribed marks incorporating the initials TB as found on plate with London marks ranging from 1621–1622 to 1662–1663, the proper time frame for Thomas Berry's life.[6] One of these in particular may be his maker's mark. It is a cursive TB in monogram with pellets on either side in a shield, and the letters bear a close resemblance to the upper case initial letters in Berry's signature on his will in the Oxfordshire Archives. Jackson shows this mark on a Communion cup of 1631–1632 at St. Dunstan's, Stepney, and on a Communion paten at Wootton Bassett, Wiltshire.[7] Pickford adds the following for the same maker's mark but without location: a chalice and paten of 1640–1641, a Communion flagon and a flat-top tankard of 1655–1656, a Communion flagon of 1660–1661, and a cup hallmarked 1662–1663.[8] Since only the two large pieces were mentioned by Berry as having gone up to London and

[4]Jesus College Buttery Accounts.

[5]New College, 1139–1149.

[6]Sir Charles James Jackson, *English Goldsmiths and Their Marks* (1921). Revised by Ian Pickford in 1989.

[7]Jackson, 118.

[8]Pickford, 115.

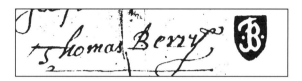

Signature of Thomas Berry on his will. Copyright
Oxfordshire Archives. Reproduced with permission.
His possible mark is shown at the right.

back to Oxford, it can be assumed the smaller pieces were not sent for assay, therefore left unmarked or marked only with the maker's mark.

The work recorded at Exeter, Jesus, and New Colleges appears to be
the sum total of Thomas Berry's employment by the Oxford colleges. No
certain statement can be made, however, because more than a few of the
college records from the seventeenth century are missing or are sketchy in
their content. The University, though, entrusted him with the mending of
"Mr. Langley's staffe" in 1656–1657, for which he was paid 10s.[9]

Most of Thomas Berry's activities centered around local politics. As
early as 1628, he was elected to the Common Council of the City, and then
recommended by the Mayor as his chamberlain and subsequently approved. The election was 2 October and four days later he paid 3s. 4d. for
not being constable. While serving as chamberlain he was elected keykeeper as well in 1636. He was reelected chamberlain for many years, but
before his term beginning 30 September 1642 was over, he was in trouble.

Less than a month after the election, Charles I made Oxford his head-
quarters, taking up residence in Christ Church College. On 10 September
1643, the King, then at Shrewsbury Castle, wrote a letter to the Mayor
of Oxford stating that he understood there were several aldermen and Common Council members who had left the City many months previously, as
the King put it, "to join the rebellion." The Council thought it reasonable
to follow the King's recommendation (not that they had any real choice),
and disenfranchise the thirteen men whom they regarded as "evilly disposed
toward the King." They were accordingly made to forfeit the freedom of the
City and were deprived of their offices. Thomas Berry was one of them.[10]
Where he went is unknown—perhaps to Chipping Norton. His absence
from the City obviously interfered with his goldsmithing business.

[9]Oxford University Archives, WPB/21/4.
[10]*OCA, 1626–1665,* 114–115.

Two and a half years later, on 29 June 1646, after the City had surrendered to the Parliamentarians under Sir Thomas Fairfax, the Act which had been requested by His Majesty was repealed and the errants were restored to their privileges and offices. Then 1 October Berry was again elected chamberlain, and the following year keykeeper. Perhaps he was fortunate to have been absent from the city as Oxford was visited by camp fever in 1643 and plague the following year. His time away from Oxford, though, may not have been too agreeable to his health as 1 November 1647, Council agreed to allow him to come to their meetings wearing his cloak, but such permission was granted only until the next Lady Day [25 March].[11] He must have been feeling the cold more than usual.

Berry rose to be one of the eight Assistants 12 September 1648. A little more than a fortnight later he was on the Mayor's Council. On 2 May 1650 the House unanimously agreed to give additional powers to Thomas Berry and four others to meet with commissioners appointed by the University "to examine into differences between the City and the University" which were before a Parliamentary committee for regulating the University. He was elected to the Mayor's Council 1 October on which he continued for a number of years. In 1654 he was defeated by Lord Whitlock to represent the City in Parliament by a vote of 155 to 85.[12]

With the defeat of the monarchy came the need to replace the late King's arms with those of the Commonwealth. Oxford was slow in complying with the Act of Parliament regarding the alteration of all maces within the Commonwealth, and the removal of the King's arms in all places. The Council finally got around to it at the beginning of 1651/2 when they ordered the royal arms in the Guildhall taken down. On 3 January they appointed Thomas Berry and "Mr. Bailiffe Wright" [William Wright, goldsmith] to see to it that the arms on the great mace were exchanged. They also had instructions "that the silver Mace now remayning in the chest in the Auditt howse bee taken forth and made the best of, and the moneyes that shall be made thereof shall bee imployed in the chardge of making up the great mace and what chardges more shall be necessary to be expended thereupon shall bee paid out of the Treasure of this City . . ."[13]

[11]*Ibid.*, 203.
[12]*Ibid.*, 152.
[13]*Ibid.*, 182.

It is difficult to sort out exactly what was done, but apparently another mace, either an older or lesser one [the one in the Audit House] was to be sold or melted to provide funds for the alteration of the Great Mace. It is probable that the mace was melted and the silver used to refashion only the portion of the Great Mace emblazoned with the royal arms as the key-keepers' accounts show a payment of £2/6/0 was made to Thomas Berry and William Wright "toward the payment of the new mace."[14] It is reasonable to assume that these two goldsmiths did the work.

By 1657 Thomas Berry was a keykeeper and the following year a gentleman assistant on the Mayor's Council. Two years later he was again one of the eight Assistants, but was not told of the Council meeting so was permitted to take the oath of allegiance in the Mayor's office 25 May 1660. By September, however, it was deemed that his election was irregular as he had been elected from a chamberlain's place and had not been Mayor and this was contrary to custom. The £5/0/0 he had paid upon election was repaid and his political career thus came to an end.[15]

It will be recalled that Thomas Berry had been apprenticed to Walter Wilkins and as such had lived in his household at No. 119 High Street. This, along with No. 118, was originally the western portion of a medieval dwelling called "Redcocks" which the City had purchased from Oriel College in 1419. During the seventeenth century they were always leased together. Wilkins died in 1623, four years after Berry was granted his freedom, and it is likely that he continued to live there,[16] as in a lease of 1634 he is mentioned as being at this address.[17] Undoubtedly he was carrying on his trade at the shop in the front of the ground floor of No. 119 which at that time was leased separately from New College to which it belonged.[18]

The widow of Walter Wilkins remarried thus becoming Jane Pope. Two years after her death the lease passed to her father, the Reverend John Dod of Fawsley, Northamptonshire, on 10 May 1637. Berry was occupying both Nos. 118 and 119, and then he became the lessee 30 April 1652, with his lease being renewed 6 June 1665. He paid £2/0/0 rent to

<hr />

[14]*Ibid.*, 436.

[15]*Ibid.*, 224 *et passim.*

[16]Catherine Cole, "The Wall Paintings at No. 118 High Street, Oxford: A Possible Attribution," Appendix to E. C. Rouse, "Some 16th and 17th Century Domestic Paintings in Oxford," *Oxoniensia*, XXXVII (1972), 205–207.

[17]Salter, *Oxford City Properties* (1926) 129.

[18]Cole, *loc. cit.*, 206.

the City 25 March 1658, when he was listed in the Southeast Ward, All Saints parish, which encompasses the High Street address.[19] In the Poll Tax of 1667, Berry paid £1/1/0 which was the rate for a gentleman, and was assessed 3s. for his wife and two daughters. In the subsidy of the same year he paid 4s. whereas in the Subsidy of 1648 his tax had been 3s.[20]

No record of Thomas Berry's marriage has been found either in All Saints, Oxford, or St. Mary the Virgin, Chipping Norton. It is probable that his wife whose name was Sara _____, was from a place other than Oxford and the wedding would have been solemnized in her home parish. There is always the possibility, though, that the record simply did not make its way into the parish register. There is the record, however, of eight children baptized at All Saints: Sarah, 26 December 1628; Thomas, 2 December 1630; Amy, 20 September 1632; Benjamin, 15 March 1634/5; Roberta, 4 October 1636; Mary, 22 January 1638/9; Amos, 10 April 1641, and Hannah, 25 February 1642/3. Thomas lived only briefly, being buried 23 June 1631.

When Berry wrote his will in 1661, the only children named were Benjamin as the eldest son, and Sarah the eldest daughter, Amos, Rebeckah who may have been the same daughter as Roberta in the baptismal register, and Esther his youngest daughter who does not appear in the baptismal register. Also named was a granddaughter, Sarah Attkins, probably the child of Sarah.[21] In those days of rather appalling child mortality it is likely all the others predeceased their father.

Thomas Berry was seventy-five years old when he died, being buried at All Saints 14 April 1670. It was more usual in the seventeenth century and earlier not to write one's will until the end was drawing near as to do otherwise was regarded as a harbinger of death. Nearly nine years had elapsed since he had signed it 12 June 1661, but in it he did not make the usual observations about being weak in body but sound in mind. When his political career ended in 1660, and he seems not to have been a working goldsmith, perhaps he felt life was over. As a matter of fact he does not describe himself as "goldsmith" in his will, nor are the tools of his craft mentioned in this document nor in the inventory of his estate. There is record of his having taken only two apprentices: William Gough in 1620 and Samuel Wilkins in 1632, plus Obediah Lord who was turned

[19]*Ibid.;* Salter, *op. cit.,* 127, 10.
[20]Salter, *Surveys and Tokens* (1923), 228, 166.
[21]Oxon. Archives, W. I. 6/4/7.

over to him after the death of Walter Wilkins. After an extraordinarily long and pious preamble which was generally the mark of a Puritan, he gets down to the mundane business of disposing of his worldly estate.

To the poor of the parish of Chipping Norton he left the sum of 40s. to be distributed by his kinsman, Robert Berry,[22] and Anthony Smith, tanner, both of the same parish, and to the poor of All Saints, Oxford, 10s. His wife was to nominate ten poor widows living in the city of Oxford or suburbs to receive 10s. each. Benjamin was bequeathed £5/0/0, and Amos £40/0/0. His granddaughter, Sarah Attkins, received £5/0/0 "as a remembrance of my love to her." These legacies were to be paid from the rents derived from his lease of 118/119 High Street. This lease which he held from the City of Oxford was bequeathed to his three daughters to be divided by a complicated formula based on their seniority. Whether to sell the lease or renew it was left to the discretion of them and their mother. His loving wife was named executrix and was bequeathed the remainder of his estate.

Thomas Berry added a Memorandum to his will 29 March 1670 to clarify the matter of the lease. His wife was instructed not to sell the lease until "Dan: Porter's time be expired, that is to say, for the space of three years & three Quarters."[23] Accordingly, 3 June 1674, the lease passed to Daniel Porter, goldsmith, stating that the premises were now in his tenure, and the bounds and rent were to remain as before.[24] Evidently the Berry family sold the lease to Porter, and there are no further records of Thomas Berry's family.

The Hearth Tax of 1665 showed Thomas Berry being assessed for four hearths at 119 High Street, and Daniel Porter for two hearths in All Saints parish, Southeast Ward, High Street. This would have been 118 High Street.[25] The inventory of Berry's estate which was made 21 April 1670, in which he is described as goldsmith, provides a superb picture of what 119 High Street and its furnishings were like when he occupied it.

The hall contained one table, one court cupboard, one round table, three leather stools, two chairs, andirons, fire shovel and tongs with a

---

[22]He was probably the son of Thomas Berry, gentleman, who was baptized 8 August 1602, and Margett Fowler, his wife. Thomas was probably the brother of Richard Berry, mercer, father of Thomas Berry, goldsmith. *Vide* Chipping Norton Parish Register Transcript.

[23]Oxon. Archives, W. I. 6/4/7.

[24]Salter, *Oxford City Properties,* 127.

[25]Salter, *Surveys and Tokens,* 201.

total value of £1/5/0, and two old striped carpets valued at 2s. The kitchen contained pewter listed at £2/0/0 and brass at £1/0/0, one safe, one table and one round table, 10s.; four low chairs and five stools worth 5s.; one jack, three spits and three jack weights, £1/10/0; two tin dripping pans and one roaster, 2s.; two old iron pots, 5s.; three spinning wheels valued at 1s. each, and other small utensils, 3s. The kitchen chamber had one chair, three stools, and one clos. stool [closet stool] worth 10s. The kitchen, no doubt, was the center of family life.

The hall chamber was well furnished with one bedstead, one trundle-bed, one flockbed, two bolsters, three pillows, four blankets, one old rug, and one old coverlet with a total value of £2/6/0. There were two chests, three chairs, two low stools, and three cushions valued at 15s.; one pair little dogs and one fire shovel, 2s., and one table, 3s. 6d. Other furnishings in the room were one looking glass and two oiled curtains, 4s.; eleven pairs of sheets and one odd sheet worth £2/17/6; six pairs of pillowbeers [pillow cases?], 12s.; four dozen napkins, hemp and flaxen, £1/0/0; twelve tablecloths, £1/4/0; one and a half dozen towels hemp and flaxen, 18s., and two cupboard cloths, 5s.

In the entry chamber were two featherbeds, two bolsters, one flock bolster with a value of £5/0/0; one rug and one blanket, 15s.; one set of old curtains, valents [valences] and carpet, £1/5/0; one chair and four low stools, 12s.; one bedstead, flockbed and bolster, 10s. Even the cockloft contained one trundlebed and three old curtains valued at 5s.

From the inventory only three hearths can be identified: in the hall, the kitchen, and the hall chamber. Perhaps one of the larger rooms had two fireplaces. At least some of the rooms must have been quite ample to accommodate the 29 chairs and stools, five tables, all those bedsteads and other articles of furniture.

Thomas Berry's wearing apparel was valued at £5/0/0; plate and money, £10/0/0; books, £1/0/0, and fuel, tubs, and lumber, £1/0/0. The lease of his house valued at £300 brought the total worth of his estate to £344/1/0.[26] It appears that the Berry family lived quite well by the standards of the day.

[26]Oxon. Archives, W. I. 6/4/7.

William Gough

William Gough (also spelled Goffe), son of William Gough of the City of Oxford, tailor, was apprenticed to Thomas Berry of the City of Oxford, goldsmith, 12 September 1620.[1] He received his freedom 17 September 1627, and it was recorded again 22 September 1628. His father had been admitted free 19 March 1613 for a payment of 40s. and the fees of 4s. 6d. and 2s. 6d.[2]

There is no record of any work done by him; however, he did take part in City government. In 1636 he was elected to the Common Council. The Mayor appointed him as his chamberlain 3 October 1637 and it was approved by the House and Commons. The following year both he and his father were chamberlains, and 30 September 1642, William Gough, Jr. was again chamberlain.[3] In the Subsidy of 24 June 1648, he was assessed 2s. 6d. in All Saints parish. Widow Goffe paid 1s. in the 1667 Poll Tax and in the Subsidy of that year Mrs. Gough paid 2s. in the same parish.[4]

There is not much information about the family in Oxford parish records. William Goffe and Frances Winnutt were married at All Saints 15 November 1573. They could have been the grandparents of William the goldsmith. William Goffe, [Sr.] gave 3s. 4d. toward a subscription for clock and chimes in 1619 at St. Martin's as found in the Churchwardens' Accounts. Richard, son of William Gough, was baptized 28 March 1631. A daughter, Elizabeth, was christened 24 May 1635, both at All Saints. With this the Gough family disappears from the registers.

There was a large Gough family of goldsmiths at Marlborough whose patriarch was William Gough I. They were prosperous well into the

---

[1]Hanaster Book, 1613–1640, L.5.2.
[2]*OCA, 1626–1665*, 225.
[3]*Ibid.*, 71 *et passim*.
[4]Salter, *Surveys and Tokens*, 231, 339.

eighteenth century.[5] Richard Gough, gentleman, merchant of Bristol, was buried 5 August 1629, at St. Mary the Virgin, Oxford. There is, however, no known connection with William Gough, Oxford goldsmith.

[5] *Vide* T. A. Kent, *West Country Silver Spoons and Their Makers, 1550–1750* (1992), 93–94.

Daniel Porter, Sr.

Daniel Porter, Sr., was the son of a London goldsmith, William Porter, and was baptized 14 April 1630, at St. Matthew, Friday Street, London. He apparently had a sister, Joyce, baptized there 29 September 1627, and buried 3 August 1629. A brother, John, was buried in the Church of St. Vedast, Foster Lane, 3 December 1649. From other documents it is known that he had another sister, Mary, whose baptismal record has not been found.

William Porter, son of John Porter, yeoman of Wirke [?] in the parish of Radley, Berkshire, was first apprenticed to Agmundisham Pyckayes in 1613, but four years later he was turned over to Mathew King 31 March 1617, and received his freedom 8 March 1621/2.[1] William was buried in the new churchyard of St. Vedast 9 March 1653/4.[2] His master, Mathew King, had been buried at St. Vedast 4 July 1623.

William Porter took four apprentices: Nathaniel Thompson, 1623; William Paterick [Patrick], 1631; James Emery, 1644, and Raph [Ralph] Bagley, 1649.[3] During these years Daniel left London for Oxford to be apprenticed to William Wright 13 September 1645.[4] There is no evidence to explain why he did not choose to be apprenticed to his father. The term of his apprenticeship was nine years at the end of which he was to receive from his master double apparel (two suits of clothes) which was customary. Apprenticeships could be for a term of seven to ten years.

---

[1]Goldsmiths' Company Apprenticeship Book I, p. 214; Court Minute Book 14a, p. 146.

[2]William Porter, goldsmith, is not to be confused with William Porter, cutler, who held a lease from the Goldsmiths' Company of a tenement in Shoe Lane. This William Porter died in the year of the plague and his property was burned in the Great Fire. He was buried 20 December 1664 at St. Bride's Church. (St. Bride's Parish Register, London Guildhall MS. 13771).

[3]Goldsmiths' Company Apprentice Book I, pp. 261, 303, 374; Apprentice Book II, p. 34.

[4]Hanaster Book, 1639–1662, L.5.3.

Daniel Porter chose to stay on in Oxford and was admitted to the liberty of the City 15 September 1654,[5] marking the beginning of an active life of forty years during which he was not only a busy goldsmith, but also a banker, pawnbroker, dealer in rare coins, politician, and a frequenter of the local taverns. The first mention of any of these pursuits was 11 March 1657/8 when he sold medals and a brass coin to Anthony Wood for 10d., and 3 November Wood paid him 3s. 6d. for drawing arms, then 12 September 1659, 8d. for a Roman coin.[6] One wonders where Porter obtained the coins—perhaps by doing some digging in the Cotswolds.

Also in 1659, Porter makes his first appearance as a goldsmith to the colleges when he was paid £22/13/6 by Christ Church for five college pots.[7] These were a type of porringer, bulbous and squat with large ring handles on either side at the narrowed neck, and used for beer in the college halls. There are no records to indicate what he was doing in those five years between the gaining of his freedom and 1659. It is possible that he was engaged in work for private citizens and, unfortunately, no records of such are extant. He also may have been working as a journeyman for his former master, William Wright.

Pembroke College required those receiving payment from the college to sign the Bursar's Book stating they had been paid, but by 1722 this procedure had been abandoned. Accordingly, 3 November 1660, Daniel Porter signed for 6s. 6d. paid to him for mending college plates. It should be pointed out that the frequent mention of "plates" in most of the college records did not necessarily mean plates as such. It was a generic term covering all sorts of silver objects, just as the term "plate" is used today. Porter's work for Pembroke was sparse. It was sixteen years before his signature appears again. Then on 3 July 1676, he was paid £1/3/6 for changing and engraving plates. Fourteen shillings was the cost of mending and exchanging college plates 9 May 1683,[8] and his name does not appear again.

Jesus College paid him 18s. for unspecified work in 1669, and in 1672, the Buttery Accounts note, "To Porter the Goldsmith for change and mending of Plate in severall years preceding £4/9/1." New College paid him 13s. in 1664, and the following year 12s. 8d. for the changing and

[5]Ibid.
[6]Wood, *Life and Times,* I, 264, 281.
[7]Christ Church College xii.b.102.
[8]Pembroke College 4.3.1.

mending of plate. His bill in 1666 of 18s. 6d. was again for mending.[9] Apparently the only work done for All Souls occurred 18 December 1687 when he was paid 9s. 6d., and 4 January 1689/90, when the bill was 2s. 6d.[10] The work is not described but judging by the small amounts, it would have been for repairs. All Souls, not having students, would not have had as much need for goldsmiths.

Magdalen College seems to have had more work for goldsmiths than any of the other colleges with the possible exception of Brasenose. It was at Magdalen that Daniel Porter had the most consistent employment from 1662 to 1694, the last year of his life.[11] The first payment to him by the college was for repairing and altering a silver vessel and for silver spoons (presumably for making the latter) at a cost of £2/18/2. Repairing and refashioning existing pieces formed the bulk of his work, and the largest payment in all those years was £16/8/0 in 1683.[12]

Porter did a considerable amount of reworking and refashioning silver for use other than in Hall, some of it for the President's Lodgings. Looking back 300 years it is difficult to sort out from the entries in the college accounts whether specific names mentioned refer to current Fellows or to past donors of the plate in question. They may be some of each. Only those who kept the records would know. As an example, "Bickley's Tankard weighing twenty-nine ounces & one half being much bruised and broken was deliver'd to Mr. Porter Goldsmith, to be changed for some plates for ye Presidents Lodgings, & to have the same inscription & Armes engraven upon them." It is rather obvious here that Bickley was the original donor. Reference is made, however, to a gilt bowl and cover "that was bought for Dr. Goodwin's use." It went into the melting pot. Another tankard, in 1666, was deemed to be of bad fashion and was turned over to Porter to be exchanged for one of better fashion.[13] In changing some of these pieces the new ones sometimes weighed less than the original, so part payment was made in the left-over silver which explains the relatively small cash amounts entered in the accounts.

[9]New College Custus Butlariae, 4219, 4220, 4221.

[10]All Souls DD c.364.

[11]It is not always possible to separate Daniel Porter, Sr. from Daniel Porter, Jr., in the bursar's entries at Magdalen and other colleges.

[12]Magdalen College LCE30, 31, 32.

[13]E. Alfred Jones, *Catalogue of the Plate of Magdalen College*, Oxford (1940), documents transcribed, 95–96.

The only mention of Daniel Porter at Corpus Christi College was in 1671 or 1672 when he was paid £6/9/0 for two college pots weighing twenty-one ounces.[14] At Oriel he began working for the college in 1662 when he was paid 15s. His name does not appear again until 1666 with the payment of £2/10/4. The following year there is a curious entry for 17s. 3d. paid to Samuel Wilkins and Daniel Porter implying that they were working together. Wilkins had been apprenticed to Thomas Berry and Porter to William Wright, so it was not a master-apprentice relationship. The last payment to Porter was made in 1687—for 5s. Over the years the amounts ranged from 4s. to £2/16/0 with the exception of £9/17/6 paid to him in 1669. It is unfortunate that not once was the kind of work done specified.[15] Porter's first work at Balliol was in 1668. He did mending of silver in 1671, and was employed again in 1675, 1683 and 1688.[16] At the end of December 1673, he signed a receipt at University College for £5/0/0 received in payment of work done for Thomas Laurence, a Fellow of the college,[17] and in 1682, he mended some plates at Wadham for £1/8/0.[18] Apparently his only business deal with the University was 12 November 1686 when the Chancellor's Court Register records the sale to Porter of three cups, one bodkin, four rings and two pieces of gold for which the University received £5/17/0.[19]

Daniel Porter's political career was unspectacular. In 1660 he was on the Common Council and had a chamberlain's place as the Mayor's child.[20] Eight years later he again had a chamberlain's place, and in 1679, a bailiff's place. He apparently tired of politics as 3 August 1680, the Mayor reported to the Council that Mr. Porter had promised to present to the City a piece of plate valued at £20 if they would "not elect him to any office or place in the Council Chamber in future." The deal was accepted by an act of Council. Porter wasted no time in fulfilling his promise as on 13 September the Mayor delivered for the use of the City a large silver basin weighing 70 oz. 4 dwt. which was engraved with the arms of

[14]Corpus Christi Libri Magni C/24/2/Box 1.
[15]Oriel College Treasurers' Accounts.
[16]Balliol College Liber Bursarii.
[17]University College MS.
[18]Wadham College 16/2.
[19]University Archives, 1686/76:1.
[20]To be a Mayor's child simply meant that the appointment was in the hands of the Mayor.

the City and which had been given to him by Daniel Porter.[21] In 1794 the City decided to sell it and the decision was entered in the Council Acts: "March 28, 1794. A silver bowl, which was the gift of Mr. Porter, is to be sold and a silver table dish with his name engraved thereon is to be purchased instead for the use of the Mayor, and the extra expense to purchasing the same and of another dish for the same purpose shall be paid by the City Treasurer and allowed in his accounts."[22]

It is not known if Daniel Porter actually made the bowl or if he purchased it from a London goldsmith and then did the engraving of the Oxford city arms, but it must have been a magnificent piece. Why the City chose to sell it is a mystery. No mention is made of it being battered or out of fashion and therefore undesirable.

In 1660 he was a member of the committee regarding the acquisition of a new Great Mace.[23] This committee and the gift of the bowl in 1680 are the only records of the City utilizing Daniel Porter's goldsmithing. Other Oxford goldsmiths received frequent commissions from the Council, but it must be admitted there was a bit of nepotism in that.

Porter, like others in the craft, kept shop, and of course there is no record of those retail transactions. For all of them the making of gold rings and silver bodkins was a staple. In 1686, on November 10 he was made to appear before the Court of the London Goldsmiths' Company for selling a gold ring worse than standard for which he was ordered to pay the cost of the ring plus a fine of £4/6/0. The ring was then returned to him defaced.[24] Two years later, on 25 July, there is mention of him again in the Court Minute Books, but this time he is not the guilty party. Two other men, one a goldsmith and the other presumably so, were involved in the distribution of substandard goods and were summoned to the Court. George Church, place of residence not stated but probably London, had made "divers gold earrings for one Mr. Hawson" who in turn sold them to Daniel Porter. Church was fined £2/10/0 and was ordered to pay Porter for the merchandise which he promised to do. It seems that Hawson was left holding the bag. The entry in the Minute Book is somewhat confused

---

[21]*OCA, 1666–1701,* 127–128.

[22]*OCA, 1752–1801,* 222. The Treasurer's Accounts are not extant, so there is no further record of the transaction. Neither did the bowl pass through Sotheby's or Christie's salerooms. It may have been sold to a local goldsmith for scrap.

[23]*Vide* account of this in "John Slatter."

[24]Goldsmiths' Company Court Minute Book 9, p. 172a.

as in the first instance the name Dubber (also an Oxford goldsmith) is crossed out and Porter written in, but not in the second instance. It is presumed, however, that Porter was the victim, not Dubber.[25]

Thanks to Anthony Wood, who might be called the town gossip, something is known of Porter's other activities. They apparently enjoyed each other's company in the conviviality of the local taverns. Between 1661 and 1668, Wood records visits with him to the Crowne Tavern, the Mermaid, and the Floure de luce [Fleur de lys]. They attended a funeral at Iffley and afterwards stopped at Earles for "strong waters." Wood also mentions paying Dan Porter 4d. for his shoe buckles.[26]

Traditionally, goldsmiths were also bankers, and Daniel Porter was no exception, or perhaps it would be more appropriate to call him a pawnbroker. Wood dined with the bursar of Magdalen on Sunday, 4 March 1687/8, who told him that the Fellows of the college had pawned most of the college plate to Dan Porter for £700—money needed to carry on their controversies with the Ecclesiastical Commissioners. The sum of £700 turned out to be an exaggeration, the actual amount being only £150.[27]

Daniel Porter continued living for the remainder of his life at 118-119 High Street, and in 1667 he was one of the two assessors for All Saints parish for the Poll Tax. He is listed as having £100 in money and paid a tax of £1/1/0, the rate for a gentleman. Three shillings were paid for his wife and two children. Also in the household was Mary Pope with wages of 30s. who paid 2s. She must have been a servant, but it is curious that one with that surname should be resident in the house previously occupied by Jane Wilkins Pope. In the Subsidy of that same year Porter paid 5s. In 1665 he was taxed for two hearths.[28]

In the register of St. Michael-at-the-North Gate is the marriage of Daniel Porter of All Saints, Oxford, and Jane Ayleworth of West Hanny, Berkshire. The ceremony was performed by Thomas Dennis, Mayor, on January 8, 1657/8. Their son, George, was baptized at All Saints 12 April 1661, and going on two years later Daniel married again. There is no record of Jane's burial in Oxford, so it is likely that she was buried at West Hanny. January 1, 1662/3 Daniel Porter and Mary Hayward (mistakenly

[25]Court Minute Book 10, p. 5.
[26]Wood, *Life*, I, 399, 439; II, 145; I, 421; II, 117.
[27]*Ibid.*, III, 258.
[28]Salter, *Surveys and Tokens*, 228, 339, 201.

given as Haywood in the parish register) were married at All Saints. Three children were born of this marriage.

George, the son by the first marriage, was apprenticed to his father for seven years 13 April 1677,[29] but he is mentioned only once in other records and then not by name when he allegedly engraved a seal in 1692/3 for Anthony Wood.[30] He was buried at All Saints 20 December 1693, at the age of 32.

Daniel Porter, Jr., destined to be a wealthy goldsmith, was born circa 1664; William, circa 1667/8, and Mary was baptized at All Saints 28 September 1675. William matriculated in Oxford University from Magdalen Hall 27 March 1685, age 17, received his B.A. degree in 1689, M.A., 1691, and B.Med., 1694. In the matriculation register his father is described as "gentleman."[31] William practiced medicine in Nottingham, and was married there in the parish of St. Peter to Elizabeth Porter of Bingham November 22, 1699. The license describes him as a 32-year-old bachelor M.D.[32]

Daniel Porter, Sr., died suddenly in his bed in the morning of Wednesday, 14 November 1694, at the age of 64,[33] and was buried at All Saints eight days later. His wife had been buried there 8 June 1686. Porter wrote his will 20 January 1693/4 describing himself as "Daniel Porter the elder of the City of Oxford Goldsmith," and going on to say that he was "in health of body and of good and perfect memory," but apparently he was not as healthy as he thought. He commended his body to be decently buried at the discretion of his executor, and then moved on to his worldly goods.

The dwelling house "scituate against All Saints Church in Oxford" was left to his eldest son Daniel with the instruction that he was to renew the lease from the City of Oxford at the usual times throughout his natural life, then after his decease it was to pass to his son William if he were still alive. Daniel was also to receive one-half of all the household goods except all the plate and all other things relating to his trade; these he was to receive in full as well as all other goods and chattels not otherwise disposed of by previous bequests. The other half of the household goods was bequeathed to his son William and daughter Mary Porter to be divided

[29]Hanaster Book, 1662–1699, L.5.4.
[30]Wood, *Life*, IV, 33.
[31]Foster, *Alumni Oxoniensis, 1500–1714*, 1183.
[32]Nottingham Marriage Licenses, Archdeacon's Court.
[33]Wood, *Life*, III, 472.

between them at the discretion of his mother-in-law, Mary Hayward, and his sister-in-law, Anne Hayward. In other words, they were to be the referees in case of a dispute.

William was to receive £40 yearly paid to him by Daniel for ninety-nine years if William lived that long; and, Mary was to pay him £10 yearly from a copyhold in Binsey. William was also bequeathed £500 to be paid to him one year after the decease of his father along with £20 interest on the money.

To his daughter Mary, Daniel left all those "Lands grounds meadows and other the premises and appurtenances thereunto belonging" lying in Binsey and held by lease of three lives from the Dean and Chapter of Christ Church Cathedral then in the tenure or occupation of Thomas Cruch of Medley, Oxon. After her death these lands were to pass to the heirs of her body. If there were none then Daniel and William were to be the beneficiaries. Mary also was bequeathed £500 plus £20 interest. One hundred pounds was willed to his granddaughter, Anna Maria Porter, to be paid to her when she was twenty-one years old.

Other heirs were Daniel's in-laws, Mary and Anne Hayward, who were given £5/0/0 each to buy mourning. His sister, Mary Robinson, was left £4/0/0 yearly to be paid throughout her life, and her daughter was willed £5/0/0 to be paid a month after his decease. A like amount was to be distributed to the poor of All Saints parish by his sole executor, Daniel Porter, Jr. The will was probated in the Prerogative Court of Canterbury 27 March 1695.[34]

[34]P.R.O., P.C.C. Will [37 Irby] Prob. 11/424.

Daniel Porter, Jr.

No baptismal record has been found for Daniel Porter, Jr., but from other sources it can be determined that he was born circa 1664. The seven-year apprenticeship to his father was entered 16 April 1679,[1] and nothing much is known of him until he appears in the Council Acts as causing trouble for the authorities.

January 28, 1695/6, it was decided that the chamberlains were to take the serjeants to assist them in shutting down his shop window. The complaint was that he was keeping an open shop window without being a freeman, and this was illegal. He could have received his freedom by patrimony, but evidently had not bothered to do so as he was working for his father. Now, however, his father was dead, and apparently the action taken by the authorities went unheeded—presuming the order was carried out.

A fortnight later the City Fathers were still wrestling with the problem as on 8 March an alderman, both bailiffs, and the mace bearer were to inspect the City by-laws regarding such matters and to proceed as they thought fit to force compliance. They seem to have been persuasive as a week later Daniel Porter, Jr., was admitted to the freedom of the City and paid the usual fees. The following 30 September he was chosen to fill up the 24, and on 3 December he paid 3s. 4d. for not being constable. The same year he had a chamberlain's place.[2]

Young Porter had a decidedly stubborn streak. On the same day he paid his fine for not being constable, Council decided that the High Steward of the City was to be informed as soon as possible that he was refusing "to pay £2/13/4 in lieu of entertaining the house and also for

---

[1]Hanaster Book, 1662–1699, L.5.4.
[2]OCA, 1666-1701, 252–253.

not entertaining the commons."[3] It seems that he had no more taste for politics than his father had had, and he played no further part in the government of Oxford. He did, however, serve as a vestryman of All Saints parish.[4]

His work for the colleges was not extensive. Exeter paid "Mr. Porter" £1/0/0 for six years of mending college plate. The entry in the bursar's book is undated and as it appears between an entry of 1696–1697 for the donation of 10s. to prisoners in the Bocardo and one for payment to Mr. Dubber in 1701–1702, it cannot be ascertained which Mr. Porter had done the work. Daniel Porter, Jr., signed the bursar's book at Pembroke 15 October 1687 receipting the payment of 19s. for mending several plates. Ten years later Jesus College paid him £8/11/0 for "Thomas Lewis, Esq. Plate."[5] Jesus was very sparse with descriptions. "Mr. Porter" was paid by Magdalen in 1696, but no amount was entered, and the following year he was paid £3/18/0, but for what is not specified.[6]

He probably found banking more to his liking. Anthony Wood noted that between 9 January and 22 April 1695 the 80 guineas he had given him at 2s. per guinea had risen to 5s. In that same year he had given him £112 for an annuity of £12.[7] Porter's biggest recorded transaction was made with New College. Under date of 21 December 1695.

> Four hundred & eighty six Spur-royals, and other six pieces of gold were taken out of the Treasury; all which pieces of gold were delivered to Mr. Porter, goldsmith, for seven hundred pounds to be repaid to the seven senior Fellows, Trustees chosen by the college to be by them laid out or returned to the Treasury, as Mr. Warden & the Society shall order and direct, and as it shall be thought for the public advantage of the Society, and not otherwise.
>
> The motive of thus taking down, & changing the pieces of gold aforesaid, was because of the great advance of gold, by which 193.12.6 was really added to the College stock, as appears by the following particulars.[8]

The account proceeds to list the prices of the coins. Then it was noted 14 January 1698/9 that £655/2/0 was paid into the college treasury, but that £44/18/0 was still in Porter's hands, "which is somewhat des-

[3]Ibid., 261.
[4]Oxon. Archives, D.D. Par. Oxford. All Saints a.1 (1607–1716).
[5]Jesus College Buttery Accounts.
[6]Magdalen College LCE32.
[7]Wood, Life, III, 506.
[8]New College 3506.

perate."[9] No wonder they were desperate as Porter was dead! The college had intended to use the money realized for the purchase of land or stocks.[10]

There were probably other such transactions with other clients of which no record remains. Like his father, Daniel, Jr., dealt in rare coins. When Anthony Wood died he bought part of his extensive collection.[11]

Only one other account of his activities is extant. Porter was called to testify 23 March 1692/3 in the case of Clarendon vs. Wood when Wood was on trial for libel and expulsion from the University. Daniel Porter, then described as 29 years old, was said to have engraved a seal for Wood six or seven years previously, but Porter said it had been done by his brother [George]. After some discussion of the matter, he played the diplomat, saying he equally favoured the parties litigant and wished right and justice to take place.[12]

Daniel Porter was twice married but no record of either marriage has been found. The winter of 1694–1695 was a hard winter and 25 February 1694/5 his young wife, Martha, died, only a few months after his father's death, and was buried at All Saints 5 March 1694/5.[13] She left two daughters: Anna Maria Porter was baptized 6 July 1693, and Martha Porter 2 September 1694, both at All Saints. The churchwarden's accounts of All Saints show that in 1695, 13s. 4d. was paid for Mr. Porter's grave [Daniel, Sr.] and a like amount for Mrs. Porter's [Martha]. They apparently were not residing at 118–119 High Street as in 1695 he was paying £3/0/0 per quarter rent to Anthony Wood.[14] The following year he paid 10s. tax on twenty windows or more at the High Street property[15] which he had inherited from his father and into which he had moved. The fact that the tax was levied only on the occupier proves that he was then living there.

It is not known how soon after his first wife's death that the second marriage took place, but apparently no children were born of this marriage. An affidavit was filed in the Prerogative Court of Canterbury attesting that Daniel Porter "late of the City of Oxford but in the Parish

[9]*Ibid.*
[10]New College 9469.
[11]Wood, *Life*, III, 506.
[12]*Ibid.*, IV, 33.
[13]*Ibid.*, III, 473.
[14]*Ibid.*, 482, 492.
[15]Salter, *Oxford City Properties*, 362, from MS. P.5.10 in the City Muniment Room.

of St. Paul Covent Garden in the County of Middlesex deceased," had made a will in July or August of 1697 and that it was written entirely in his own hand, signed, sealed, and executed in the presence of Thomas Collins, John Kirkson and George Walker at the deceased's home in Oxford. After Porter's death the will was publicly read in the presence of his widow, Anna Maria Porter, and delivered to her after which it was mislaid or lost.

The affidavit stated that he directed and ordered that his body should be buried in All Saints Church in Oxford near his former wife. He bequeathed £2000 to his two daughters, Anna Maria and Martha, "to be paid out of the Estate which he had with Anna Maria Porter his then wife," and after the payment of his debts the residue of his estate was left to his two daughters. Anne Hayward, his aunt, and Mary Porter, his sister, were named executrices, and they were willed £20 each for their trouble and pains. This document was probated as a will 7 July 1698.[16]

Daniel Porter, Jr., was only 33 or 34 years old when he died, and that was an early age for making a will. The circumstances surrounding his death and the disappearance of the will as well as the provisions of the will seem to indicate what today would be called a dysfunctional family. So many questions arise. What was he doing in Covent Garden, London? Had he taken suddenly ill while perhaps visiting there, or had he deserted his family? Did he perhaps commit suicide? What became of his body as there is no record of his burial at All Saints nor at St. Paul's, Covent Garden? If he were a suicide his body would have been denied church burial. The coroners' inquest reports for deaths in Middlesex at that time survive only for murders and he was not such a victim. Of course, it is possible that his burial simply did not get written down in the All Saints register. Why was his wife totally ignored in his will? After learning its contents did she deliberately destroy it rather than mislay or lose it? And finally, how did Daniel Porter, Jr., acquire such great wealth? This latter question may be answered partially by the lawsuits which were filed against him, and then following his death, against his estate in the Court of the Chancellor of Oxford University.

Daniel Porter, Jr., was pursued by his creditors in 1697, with suits brought against him in the Chancellor's Court. On January 2, 1696/7, Sir John Ludwell, M.D., of the University of Oxon. sued him

[16]P.R.O., P.C.C. Will [172 Lort] Prob. 11/496.

for £100,[17] and two days later James Badger of the University brought suit for £330.[18] Theophylus Poynter, surgeon, of the University sued him for £600 on January 20.[19] In his suit, as well as that of Badger, it was stated that Porter was suspected of fleeing to avoid appearing in court. The spectre of the Bocardo hung over him, certainly an incentive for disappearing from Oxford. It is not clear if the court action of the two medical men was related to Porter's state of health and therefore unpaid bills for their services, or if they had deposited money with Porter in relation to his banking activities. The size of the claims lends credence to the latter, and this certainly must have been true of Badger.

Law suits did not end with Porter's death. His executrices now had to contend with actions filed in the Chancellor's Court. They were sued April 26, 1699 by James Badger claiming that at the time of Daniel Porter's death he was in debt to him [Badger] for £26.[20] The following day Oriel filed a claim for an unspecified amount,[21] and the same day New College sued for £740.[22] It appears that the transaction with the spur-royals was not the only one that New College had with Porter.

The dates of these events add to the mystery surrounding the death of Daniel Porter, Jr. The three men who allegedly witnessed his will were presumably the ones who gave the undated affidavit attesting to the contents of the will which they claimed was made in July or August 1697 at his house in Oxford. If Porter had fled the City by the beginning of the year, did he quietly reappear for the purpose of writing his will? The affidavit states that it was written entirely in his own hand, and this was not usual. It may indicate the will was written in haste. Porter was dead in London by the following June or July. How long had he been there?

Daniel Porter's will had provided for the payment of his debts, a customary provision in such documents. The suits filed against him, therefore, may have been settled in this manner if he had not made restitution before his death. Badger apparently had been able to collect the major portion of the sum Porter owed him. It would seem, however, that his aunt and sister, his executrices, were not aware of the other large debts. There is no record of how these claims were settled. Mary

[17]University Archives, 1697/1:1.
[18]University Archives, 1697/3:1.
[19]University Archives, 1697/2:1.
[20]University Archives, 1699 p 13.
[21]University Archives, 1699 p 18.
[22]University Archives, 1699 p 25.

Porter[23] and Anne Hayward really earned the £20 left to each of them for "their trouble and pains." Had Anthony Wood not predeceased Porter all these questions may have been answered.

[23]Mary Porter had married sometime before April 1699 when she is described in the Chancellor's Court proceedings as the wife of William Grayhurst, a London drugster [apothecary]. The Grayhurst name does not appear in the register of St. Paul's Covent Garden.

William Robinson

It is strange that so little is known about William Robinson who was the son of Robert Robinson of the City of Oxford, gentleman. He was apprenticed to Samuel Wilkins, Oxford goldsmith, for eight years from 1 May 1659[1], which would place his birth at about 1644, presumably in Oxford.

There are, however, two entries in the register of St. Michael-at-the-North Gate, one of which may refer to him: William Robinson, son of Robert Robinson baptized 2 August 1641; and, William Robinson, son of Robert Robinson buried 1 August 1641. Presuming that the entries are correctly written, it is possible that the one baptized was named for the one buried as was often the case. As eight days normally elapsed between death and burial, the one who was buried probably had died about July 24 or 25. There is also the possibility that the dates of the entries were inadvertently reversed and that the child was baptized one day and buried the next. Another possibility is that William Robinson, goldsmith, was born circa 1644 and named for a deceased brother but that the baptism was carelessly omitted from the register.

Robinson's apprenticeship was transferred to Daniel Porter for the remainder of his term, but there is no record of his admission to the freedom of the City[2]. On 4 May 1667, he took an apprentice, Thomas Sayer, son of Lawrence Sayer, goldsmith of London, for a term of seven years.[3] His father had apprentices in London, but there is no record of his apprenticeship under the London Company. When Sayer left in 1671 nothing more is known of Robinson.[4] On June 11, 1679 a William Robinson of St. Mary Magdalen parish was buried at St. Peter-in-the-East.

[1]Hanaster Book, 1639–1662, L.5.3.

[2]Salter, *Surveys and Tokens*, 434. Salter, without explanation, names his father as being of the University of Oxford, gentleman, but nothing further has been found regarding him.

[3]Hanaster Book, 1662–1699, L.5.4.

[4]Museum of Oxford exhibit information.

June 4, 1666, William Robinson and Mary Porter were married at All Saints. The bride was the sister of Daniel Porter, Sr. There is no record of any work done by Robinson, but in 1668 he had a tradesman's token, one of which is now in the Ashmolean Museum—The obverse: Will • Robinson • 1668 = The Goldsmiths' Arms; the reverse: Govldsmith • in • Oxon = A flowering knot and W.M.R.[5] He was not listed in the Poll Tax nor the Subsidy of 1667, nor does his name appear on any leases from the City or the colleges.

As has been noted, Mary Robinson was named in Daniel Porter's will written in 1693, and no place of residence for her is stated, thus giving the impression she was still living in Oxford. This, however, cannot be taken as a positive conclusion. Mary Robinson was buried 19 February 1707/8 at St. Michael-at-the-North Gate, and another Mary Robinson was buried there 8 December 1734. She was probably the niece mentioned in Daniel Porter's will.

Robert Robynson and Joanna Mooseley were married at All Saints 6 October 1566. They may have been the parents of Robert Robinson, gentleman. William Robinson's initials on his trade token are given as W.M.R. Perhaps the M stands for Mooseley, which would have been his grandmother's maiden name. In the register of St. Michael-at-the-North Gate is the marriage March 13, 1655/6 of William Porter and Anne Robinson. This may have been another alliance between these two goldsmithing families. It is possible that William was a brother of Daniel Porter, Sr., and Anne Robinson a sister of William Robinson.

[5]Salter, *op. cit.*, 375.

Lemuel King

There is so little known about Lemuel King who left his signature on the engraving of three pieces of silver at St. John's College. More is known about his father who was a colourful character. Lemuel apparently was more subdued and conventional.

He was the son of Lawrence [or Laurence] King of the City of Oxford, glover, and was apprenticed to Daniel Porter of Oxford, goldsmith, for a term of eight years, 23 August 1672.[1] There is no record of his baptism nor his freedom, nor is it known if he married. The only office he ever held was as a vestryman of All Saints in 1687.[2] Wood mentions him only once, referring to him as King the goldsmith in whose home in All Saints parish Mary Sayer, aged about 73, died, and was buried in St. Ebbe's. Her first husband and several children had died and her second husband had deserted her and was then living in Jamaica with their son where they were merchants. She came from a Berkshire family.[3] It is not known if King had taken pity on her and she was living with him, or died there as a casual visitor.

The only evidence of his having done work for the colleges is the engraving previously mentioned, and it is a pity that there seem to be no manuscripts regarding silver earlier than the second quarter of the eighteenth century in St. John's muniments.

The three pieces he engraved were purchased from London goldsmiths. The ewer and basin given to the college by John Kent has the London hallmarks for 1685 with the maker's mark, IR above a crown. The mark is unidentified and not listed in Jackson (Pickford ed.). The basin is engraved in the center with the arms of the college in a scrolled cartouche surrounded by swags of fruit and surmounted by two winged cherubs. Below the arms

[1] Hanaster Book, 1662–1699, L.5.4.
[2] Oxon. Archives MS. D.D. Par. Oxford. All Saints a.1 (1607–1716).
[3] Wood, *Life*, III, 260.

is a wreath surrounding a lamb, a symbol of St. John the Baptist. A ribbon above the heads of the cherubs contains the block letters COLL: DI: IO: BAPT. and a ribbon below the wreath contains OXON.

The other piece is a two-handled cup or porringer presented by Sir John Pakington, Baronet, hallmarked in London in 1689, made by John Jackson who was free in 1681. It is engraved with the college arms with the cherubs at the side and the head of a cherub with wings at the top, and with Pakington's arms. The engravings are signed: L. King Sculpsit.[4] King's engraving and that of the other Oxford goldsmiths reached a standard equal to that done in London.

Twice Lemuel King was summoned to appear before the Court of the London Goldsmiths' Company. On December 22, 1686, he was charged with selling a substandard gold ring and silver bodkin, and was ordered to pay 13s., the cost of the goods, and a fine of £1/13/6 with the goods to be returned to him defaced.[5] July 18,1688, he was summoned for selling a gold ring worse than standard and was ordered to pay 5s. and the cost of the goods which was 7s. 6d. The ring was then returned to him defaced.[6]

Nothing more is known about Lemuel King, but from what is known of his father it can be imagined that he grew up in a tumultous household. Lawrence King, his father, was the son of Robert King, innholder, and was baptized at All Saints 18 November 1629. Lawrence King was a very successful glover, having been apprenticed to Thomas Meares to learn this trade 6 July 1641 for a term of eight years. By the time he gained his freedom 22 September 1651, he was described as an apprentice of John Sheene, glover. The following year he was appointed Constable of the Southeast Ward. Between 1652 and 1684, he had seventeen apprentices, and in 1654 the City paid him a total of £2/10/0 for gloves presented to the Judge at the Assize.[7] In 1667 he was listed as residing between 119 and 120 High Street in All Saints parish when he paid 7s. Poll Tax for himself, wife, and five children.[8]

---

[4]Pictured in Charles Oman, *English Engraved Silver* (1978), 69-70. Oman errs in saying that "gifts appear generally to have been sent down to the university already engraved in London." He was referring to both Oxford and Cambridge. At least at Oxford, this certainly was not true as is shown by bursars' accounts.

[5]Goldsmiths' Company Court Minute Book 9, p. 174a.

[6]*Ibid.*, 10, p. 4a.

[7]Salter, *Surveys and Tokens*, 418.

[8]*Ibid.*

Engraving signed by Lemuel King of Oxford. St. John's College, Oxford.

Lawrence King may have been baptized at All Saints, but he became a rabid Anabaptist and took to baptizing people in the river at Hythe Bridge. He and others were indicted in 1661 as being seditious and disloyal persons for attending an unlawful conventicle. They pleaded not guilty when they were already imprisoned in the Bocardo. Refusing to take the Oath of Allegiance they remained in prison until the next session with bail being denied. The following year King was indicted again, fined, and committed to the Bocardo until the fine was paid. He was indicted and fined again and again for not attending his parish church.[9] That must have been a financial strain. Various royal officials searched his house 25 June 1683 for arms. Under his new Charter James II in September 1688 ordered the City to elect Lawrence King a common councillor.[10] Perhaps by then he had seen enough of the Bacardo and was willing to submit to a more conventional lifestyle.

[9]Oxon. Archives, Petty Sessions Roll, City of Oxford, 1656-1676. O.5.11, 48–49.
[10]Salter, *op. cit.*, 418.

John Slatter

Shadowy and mysterious could describe John Slatter. He flourished very briefly and then faded ignominiously. Son of Henry Slatter of Tetsworth, Oxfordshire, yeoman, he was baptized 26 October 1617 at St. Giles, Tetsworth. October 31, 1631 he was apprenticed to Martin Wright of the City of Oxford, goldsmith, for a term of ten years, and was granted his freedom 22 September 1639.[1] His name had a variety of spellings: Slater, Slatter, Slaughter, and Sclatter, and there appears to have been more than one man in Oxford with the name of John Slatter.

Anthony Wood paid him 6d. for a Roman silver coin 5 November 1658[2], and the following year Christ Church College paid him a pound for his efforts in recovering some stolen plate.[3] During this time he was a member of the Common Council having first been elected in 1654, and re-elected in 1656, 1658 and 1660. On 22 March 1655/6, he promised to pay £4 and 3s. 4d. for not being constable.[4]

With the coming of the Restoration in 1660, the problem of the Great Mace again arose; the arms of the Commonwealth had to go. At first it was to be another alteration job, but 15 May Council decided that a new Great Mace was to be provided at the expense of the City. Like politicians today they were authorizing expenditures with no regard for means of payment. The City was out of money and was forced to borrow £100. Four members of the Council, all goldsmiths, were named to look into the matter and before making an agreement for a new mace were "to acquainte Mr. Mayor & his Brethren" with the cost. The four men

---

[1]Hanaster Books, 1613–1640, L.5.2. and 1639–1662, L.5.3.
[2]Wood, *Life,* I, 264.
[3]Christ Church MS. xii.b.102.
[4]*OCA, 1626–1665,* 206 *et passim.*

appointed were Samuel Wilkins, John Slatter, Daniel Porter, and Alexander Wright.[5]

John Slatter was a relatively minor figure, but it was he to whom the Keykeepers made payments toward the exchange of the Great Mace. Four such payments were made in 1660: £50 toward the exchange, £10 to reimburse him for what he had spent, £4/10/3 for what was due him over and above the sum of £80, and finally £20 again in repayment of money expended by him "towards the Exchange of the great Mace."[6] Since there are no hallmarks nor maker's mark visible on the mace there is no way of ascertaining with all certainty if John Slatter were actually the maker, but the lack of any marks does lend credence to the supposition that it was locally made.[7]

No mention is made in the Council Acts of the advisability of melting the old mace, and the amount of the sums expended show this was not done. The piecemeal payments to Slatter seem to indicate that he was buying silver as the work progressed. The weight of the completed mace is given as 287 ounces.[8] Presuming there is not a wooden core in the shaft, the cost of the metal and the fabrication can be determined. It is known from other documents that at about that time a goldsmith was charging 5s. per ounce for the metal and 8d. per ounce for his work. Based on these figures the cost of the silver was £71/15/0, and the cost of labour was £9/11/2, making a total of £81/6/2. John Slatter was paid £84/10/3 by the City. As engraving was always charged separately, the difference of £3/4/1 would have been for engraving the inscription in Roman capitals: THIS MACE WAS MADE IN THE MAYORALTY OF IOHN LAMBE ESQ. ANNO REGNI CAROLI 2 DUODECIMO. The mace is gilt but it must be assumed that this was done at some later time as this accounting does not allow for the cost of gilding which would have been considerable for an object 5 feet 4 inches long.

It seems rather odd the work of so fine a piece was entrusted to John Slatter, assuming that it was made by him, as the other three men of the committee were certainly more prosperous which could be a guage of

[5]OCA, 1626–1665, 260, and Council Book C, 1629–1663, A.5.7, f. 273. *Vide* Margaret Toynbee, "The City of Oxford and the Restoration of 1660," *Oxoniensia,* XXV (1961), 80–81.

[6]OCA, 1626–1665, 443.

[7]There were no marks visible on the George I mace of the Borough of Cavan, Ireland. When it was taken apart two beautifully preserved marks were found inside.

[8]Toynbee, *loc. cit.,* 80.

competence, but not necessarily so. Perhaps his design was the most pleasing and the least costly. The mace is a magnificent piece of work which leads one to wonder if Slatter were the goldsmith who made it, or if he were acting as an agent for the City in obtaining the services of a London goldsmith. It was not usual, however, for piecemeal payments to be made when a local goldsmith was acting in such a capacity.

No more is heard of John Slatter until 1663, when he petitioned the Court for the payment of £3/3/0 in arrears to him when he was overseer of the poor.[9] Five years later he was in the Bocardo. It does not appear that he was there for clipping coins; most prisoners in the gaol over the North Gate, a relic of the city's ancient fortifications, were there for debt. The Council noted 27 November 1668: "On the petition of John Slatter, a poor prisoner in the Bocardo but formerly a member of this house, to remove him to the King's Bench, it is agreed (if the Recorder advises that there will be a good return to the writ) that if Slatter brings his Habeus Corpus cum causa and removes himself thereon he shall be allowed £4."[10] It seems rather extreme to be transferred to the King's Bench, which heard civil cases, for debt, but the Quarter Sessions records for this period are not extant so there is no way of learning any other details of his incarceration.

Nothing more is known of him except that he had two sons admitted to the liberty of the City: his eldest son, John, 25 April 1662, and his third son, Yeisly, in June 1674.[11] The names of none of the family appear in the parish registers.

In the Subsidy of 1667 in the parish of St. Peter-in-the-East, John Slatter paid 1s. 4d., and in the Poll Tax of that year he was listed as having wages of £1/12/0, and paid 2s. tax.[12] Mr. Slatter was taxed for seven windows in Holywell in 1696.[13] These references may or may not be to John Slatter, goldsmith. In this latter year he would have been 79 years old.

---

[9]Oxon. Archives, Petty Sessions Roll, City of Oxford, 1656–1676. 0.5.11.
[10]OCA, 1666–1701, 28.
[11]Hanaster Book, 1662–1699, L.5.4.
[12]Salter, Surveys and Tokens, 292.
[13]OCA, 1666–1701, 362.

Richard Dubber

Richard Dubber was the senior member of a family of goldsmiths who worked in Oxford in the seventeenth and eighteenth centuries. He was the son of Richard Dubber, late of Wolvercote, Oxfordshire, yeoman, and was apprenticed 25 June 1667 to Alexander Wright of the City of Oxford, goldsmith, for a term of seven years.[1]

Wolvercote seems to have been well-populated with Dubbers judging by the number of them in the register of St. Peter's Church there, but the baptism of Richard Dubber, goldsmith, is not entered. He must have been born about 1651 or 1653 as he had three sisters, Mary, Joane and Jane, born in 1652, 1654 and 1657 respectively, all in the month of March. The first entry of Dubber to appear in the register is the baptism of William, son of Richard, October 29, 1600.

Richard Dubber was given the liberty of the City 8 June 1674,[2] and three years later he took an apprentice, Charles Badger, son of John Badger of London, cordwainer, for a term of seven years. He was entered 10 September 1677,[3] and was admitted free October 3, 1684,[4] then not seen again in the Oxford records.

Five children were born to the Dubbers, and all were baptized at St. Martin's. The eldest was Edward, baptized 18 March 1678/9. Next was Elizabeth, baptized 11 May 1681; then Timothy, 7 January 1681/2; Richard, 4 October 1682, and John christened 30 November 1683. He did not survive for long, being buried 1 or 2 December 1684. No marriage record for Richard Dubber has been found, but his wife was probably Eleanor who was buried 22 August 1689.[5]

---

[1]Hanaster Book, 1662–1699, L.5.4.
[2]*Ibid.*
[3]*Ibid.*
[4]*OCA, 1666–1701*, 166.
[5]In the parish register Timothy is listed as "son of Ed[. . .]." This should be "son of Richard."

The family moved from place to place. September 1, 1692, in a lease in St. Martin's parish to William Nicholls, dyer, with Edward Hawkes occupant of the property at Nos. 5 and 6 Queen Street, Richard Dubber is spoken of as being to the east.[6] In 1696, however, he paid tax on nine windows in a house on High Street between the Wheatsheaf at 127–129 High Street, and the Bear at 123–124 High Street in All Saints parish.[7] They moved again as in a lease of August 30, 1703, to Charles Prince for 118–119 High Street (the former home successively of Walter Wilkins, Thomas Berry, and Daniel Porter) Richard Dubber is described as being to the east. In leases of 1701 and 1715 for 117 High Street he is spoken of as being to the west.[8]

In 1679/80, Dubber was a vestryman at St. Martin's and in that year he was paid an unspecified sum for boiling and burnishing the Communion plate.[9] At All Saints, most years from 1695 to 1713 he was a member of the vestry, and for many of these years, a churchwarden as well. In 1711 the parish paid him 7s. for his journey to Burford, but the reason for the journey is not given. The following year he was paid 1s. for mending the chalice.[10]

Richard Dubber's first employment by the colleges seems to have been at All Souls when he was paid 19 October 1689 £1/7/0 for mending plate.[11] In 1701-1702, Exeter paid him £10/7/6 for "change and new making plate" but no details are given as to what the new plate was. He continued mending plate for the college through 1715 for amounts ranging from 9s. 6d. to £2/3/0.[12] From 1697 to 1704, Dubber worked for Oriel. No descriptions of the work done are recorded, but it must have been for repairs as only two payments were more than a pound.[13] Similar work was done for Pembroke in 1708, 1711 and 1714. The payment in the last year was £3/6/0, and was for mending and changing the college plate.[14]

Like a few other Oxford goldsmiths, Richard Dubber was summoned to appear before the Court of the Goldsmiths' Company for selling gold

[6]Salter, *Oxford City Properties,* 161.
[7]OCA, *1666–1701,* 348.
[8]Salter, *op. cit.,* 161.
[9]Oxon. Archives, D.D. Par. Oxford. St. Martin's a.1. (1540–1680).
[10]Oxon. Archives, D.D. Par. Oxford. All Saints a.1 (1607–1716).
[11]All Souls SS. DD. c.364.
[12]Exeter College A.II.10 (1639–1734).
[13]Oriel College Treasurer's Accounts.
[14]Pembroke College 4.3.2.

wares worse than standard. Appearing for him 26 June 1706, was "Mr. Knight" who was probably Francis Knight, an Oxford goldsmith about whom little is known. Dubber was ordered to pay £2/5/0, the cost of the goods, and a fine of £2/12/6.[15] For his next offence, 8 August of the same year a Mr. Gibbons appeared for him, again for selling gold wares worse than standard. His fine increased from the previous one to £3/16/6 plus a guinea, the cost of the goods.[16]

Richard Dubber was constable in 1679,[17] and then did not hold a city office again until 30 September 1702 when he was chosen one of the 24 in place of one who resigned. He was sworn and paid £3/10/0 for entertainment.[18] The following year he was elected a member of the Common Council. On 1 October 1705, he was chosen Mayor's Chamberlain. He and the newly elected City Chamberlain took the oaths and the outgoing chamberlain paid them £20 each, and the new ones paid 40s. each and £4 in lieu of entertainment. Dubber was then elected chamberlain every two years from 30 September 1707 to 30 September 1715, his last term ending a year before his death.[19] His name appears four times in the Council Acts (1680, 1685, 1686 and 1690) as being appointed to have £25 of Recorder Whistler's money.

Richard Dubber died intestate in 1717, and was buried 18 September 1717 at St. Mary the Virgin, Oxford. The inventory of his goods and chattels was made 18 December 1717, and his two sons, Edward and Timothy Dubber, both goldsmiths, were appointed administrators of his estate 12 September 1718.

The contents of the shop provide a picture of the sort of work he did. Twelve silver spoons were valued at £4/2/10, and a pair of silver spurs at £1/15/9. Thirty-nine gold rings were worth £19/8/0, and seven *Curralls*, which were probably corals; i.e. child's rattles or teething rings, £2/15/0. Fifteen pairs of silver buckles were appraised at £4/10/6, silver buckles and clasps at £4, and buttons, seals and old silver, £18/15/0; twenty silver stone rings at 10s., two silver cups at £2/6/9, and a silver box and two dram cups at £1/0/0. Among other items in the shop were silver boxes and

---

[15]Goldsmiths' Company Court Minute Book 10, p. 309a.

[16]*Ibid.*, 313a. Gibbons was probably John Gibbons of Foster Lane, London, whose first mark was entered as a large worker in 1700.

[17]*OCA, 1666-1701*, 121.

[18]*OCA, 1701-1752*, 16.

[19]*Ibid.*, 27 et passim.

inlaid boxes which seem to have been tortoise shell inlaid and rimmed with silver, silver thimbles, lockets, sleeve and coat buttons, earrings, tongs, needle cases, seals, a watch valued at 15s., and patterns, solder, and odd silver. There were also eighteen toy spoons and one soup spoon. A case of instruments valued at 4s. and two brushes at 3s. were probably a part of the tools of his trade but also listed were working tools and other furniture in the shop valued at £4/3/0. He also had a pair of old spectacles worth a shilling and a tobacco box at 1s. 6d.

The remainder of the inventory illustrates the rather cramped conditions in which the family lived. The kitchen contained the usual assortment of pots of brass, bell metal, and iron; a wire sieve, three chafing dishes, a skimmer, a ladle, a flour box, a warming pan, a chopping knife, a frying pan, a brass smoothing iron and six other smoothing irons, besides the customary equipment for a cooking fireplace, five candlesticks, a pair of snuffers, and a tinder box. There was pewter worth £2/17/9, which was probably what the family used for dining. The kitchen also contained a table, chairs, and joint stools valued at 5s. for the lot, and a feather bed, bolster, pillow, rug, etc., valued at £1/3/0. Three shillings was the value of a dresser and shelves.

The dining room contained three oval tables, twelve cane chairs, one stool, one stand, two cushions, a looking glass, a gun, pictures, and books. There was a fireplace in the room with the usual furnishings. The value placed on the room's contents was £7/0/10.

Another room had two pairs of stairs. It can only be surmised that one went to the cellar which had little in it, and one to a vacant loft. This room was also heated by a fireplace and contained a bedstead, a feather bed, bolster and other furnishings for the bed, eight chairs, one stool, a table, a chest of drawers, a looking glass, window curtains, pictures, and a dressing box with a total value of £6/16/6.

Richard Dubber was not as prosperous as some of the earlier Oxford goldsmiths. At his death his ready money and wearing apparel had a value of £14/2/6 and his total estate had a worth of £124/10/8.[20]

[20]Oxon. Archives, Bd. I, 107.334; 164/3/2.

Edward Dubber

Edward Dubber, eldest son of Richard Dubber, was baptized at St. Martin's 18 March 1678, and was apprenticed to his father for a term of eight years, enrolled 2 April 1691.[1] He seems to have done no work for the colleges, and his name appears only once in the City records. That was 12 August 1720, when he was to have £10 of [blank] money[2]

[1]Hanaster Book, 1662–1699, L.5.4.
[2]*OCA, 1701–1752*, 121.

Timothy Dubber

Timothy Dubber, second son of Richard Dubber, was baptized at St. Martin's 7 January 1681/2, and apprenticed to his father for seven years, being enrolled 4 October 1697.[1] The first mention of his doing work for the colleges was 4 October 1707, when he received £1/5/0 for mending college plate at Pembroke.[2] The same year he was paid a like amount by Oriel.[3] He continued to mend plate for Pembroke through 1727–1728, and the payments were usually less than a pound.[4] The same kind of work continued at Oriel through 1711 with annual payments of a few shillings.[5]

The only other college which employed him was Brasenose in 1723–1724 when he mended eleven tankards and two *stohhes* for a total of £1/11/6, but he was not paid until 8 January 1727/8.[6] There is an entry in the Court Minute Books of the London Goldsmiths' Company dated 1 October 1719, stating that Mr. Dubber of Oxford was fined £6/15/6.[7] This could have been either Edward or Timothy.

Like his elder brother, Timothy's name appears only once in the City records. He was chosen 15 September 1727 to have £25 of Sir Thomas White's money.[8] Richard Dubber and his two goldsmith sons worked together and after the father's death, the sons maintained a partnership, but they were never active in civic affairs.

[1]Hanaster Book, 1662–1699, L.5.4.
[2]Pembroke MS. 4.3.2.
[3]Oriel Treasurers' Accounts, ETC A8/12.
[4]Pembroke MSS. 4.3.2 and 4.3.3.
[5]Oriel Treasurers' Accounts.
[6]Brasenose MS. Hurst, Tradesmen's Bills 35 (1728). *Stohhes* is probably meant for stoups; i.e., basins for drinking vessels.
[7]Goldsmiths' Company Court Minute Book 12, p. 10.
[8]*OCA, 1701–1752*, 158.

Walter Wilkins

The Wilkins family goes far back into the history of Hook Norton, Oxfordshire. A Roger Wylkyns was holding lands and tenements from Oseney Manor in 1490. More than two hundred years later members of the family were still there.[1] Judging from the wills they left beginning with 1555, sheep formed the basis of the family's economy throughout the years.

Walter Wilkins, however, was the first of the family to be connected with goldsmithing and there were four to follow him in the craft. The parish registers of St. Peter's, Hook Norton, are not complete; nearly all the marriage records before 1729 have disappeared and there are obvious gaps in the baptismal records. Walter Wilkins's christening is not recorded, but he must have been born about 1584, the son of John Wilkins of Hook Norton, weaver. His mother's name is unknown. When his father wrote his will 4 March 1604/5 (probated 4 April 1608), he bequeathed to his son Walter £30, one bedstead fully furnished with bedding to it (sheets excepted), one brass pot, one kettle, one candlestick, four platters, two saucers, one pan, one broach [spit], one salt, all to be paid to him at the end of his apprenticeship.[2]

The apprenticeship of Walter Wilkins is not recorded in the Hanaster Books, but his admission to the freedom of the City 4 June 1610 is, and he is described as apprentice to William Wright, goldsmith.[3] Nearly a year previous to this event, 10 July 1609, he had taken an apprentice, Thomas Berry of Chipping Norton. His second apprentice was Obediah Lord, son of Robert Lord of Cropredy, Oxfordshire, fuller, enrolled 2 September 1618. His apprenticeship was not completed before Walter Wilkins died, so he was turned over to Thomas Berry 22 December 1623.[4] Berry had continued to live in the house at 118/119 High Street.

[1]Margaret Dickins, *A History of Hook Norton* (1928), 60.
[2]Oxon. Archives, W. 194.41; 69/4/43.
[3]Hanaster Book, 1590–1614, L.5.1.
[4]Hanaster Book, 1613–1640, L.5.2.

Obediah Lord did not stay in Oxford. In the 1666 administration of the estate of Abraham Lord of Banbury, goldsmith, who presumably was his brother, he was named as a goldsmith in Northampton. Nothing else is known of Obediah, but Abraham left an estate valued at £190/13/2 with £105 of it in gold and silver plate.[5]

Walter Wilkins soon began participating in local government. He was elected constable 2 October 1615, and on the same date in 1618, he was chosen to fill a vacancy on the Common Council. He retained that post until he was nominated 2 October 1622 by the Mayor, William Boswell, to be his chamberlain, and the appointment was "well accepted by the whole house." The following year he was again named chamberlain.[6] In 1619 he contributed 3s. 4d. to the subscription for clock and chimes at St. Martin's Church.[7]

There is little recorded of Walter Wilkins's work. A bill of 1614 at Brasenose shows that he was paid 9s. 2d. for soldering and 2s. for planishing, and scouring eight pieces for 2s. "One bowle broken in the podkin[sic] wt. 14 oz. less 6d.—3d." is also noted.[8] Four years later Oriel paid him 12d. for polishing.[9]

He did not live long enough to become well established, yet he was well known if John Aubrey is to be believed when he wrote in his *Brief Lives* that "Mr. Francis Potter knew him very well, and was wont to say that he was a very ingeniose man, and had a very mechanical head. He was much for Trying of Experiments, and his head ran much upon a *perpetual motion*."[10] Aubrey is known to have got his anecdotes mixed and attached to the wrong people, especially when suffering from a hangover. Somehow this description of Walter Wilkins seems at odds with the son of a weaver who had not really become well established before his premature death. It seems to fit better his son, John Wilkins, about whom Aubrey was writing.

Walter Wilkins married Jane Dod 28 May 1611 at St. Peter's, Hanwell. She was the daughter of the Reverend John Dod and his wife, Anne Bownde, and granddaughter of the physician to the Duke of Norfolk. Dod was a Puritan clergyman who ran into trouble with the

[5]Oxon. Archives, Peculiars 45/2/19.
[6]*OCA 1583–1626*, 247 *et passim.*
[7]Oxon. Archives, D.D Par. Oxford, St. Martin's a.1 (1540–1680).
[8]Brasenose MS. Hurst, 23.102.
[9]Oriel College Treasurer's Accounts.
[10]O. L. Dick, ed., *Aubrey's Brief Lives* (1957), 319.

ecclesiastical authorities. After serving as rector of Hanwell, Oxford-shire, from 1585 to 1604,[11] he was suspended for non-conformity and preached then at Banbury and Fenny Compton, Warwickshire, and was silenced at Canons Ashby, Northamptonshire, by Archbishop Abbot, 24 November 1611. The rest of his life was spent at the rectory of Fawsley, Northamptonshire,[12] but it would have been during his stay at Hanwell that John and Jane met as Hook Norton and Hanwell are probably not more than ten miles apart. Jane was eighteen years old at the time of the wedding, considerably younger than her husband. She was baptized, presumably by her father, 5 December 1593 at St. Peter's, Hanwell.

John Wilkins had left his son a goodly array of household goods which he was to receive at the end of his apprenticeship, but it is not known where he was living until he acquired the lease of 118/119 High Street 18 December 1618, which premises where formerly occupied by Richard Smythe. The lease was from the City of Oxford for 41 years at a rent of 40s. and two capons,[13] but his time was running out.

The 11th of February 1621/2, he wrote a short and to the point will stating that he was weak in body (his rather shaky signature would verify that), but perfect in mind and memory, and directing that his body be buried in the churchyard of All Saints. His son, John, was bequeathed £40 to be paid to him at the age of twenty-one. Daughter Mary was to receive £20 and a bed furnished worth £5/10/0. Timothy, Peter, and Martha, his other children, each were left £20. Walter willed 40s. apiece to Samuel and Margaret Wilkins, the children of his brother, Thomas. He and Timothy Dod of Hanwell were named overseers, and each were given 20s. The poor of All Saints got 10s. and another 10s. was left to the church "to bord the seats on the Northside, at the ends of them." His well beloved wife, Jane, was sole executrix.[14]

Mary was baptized 28 June 1612 at St. Peter's, Hanwell. John was born in his grandfather's house at Fawsley in 1614.[15] Peter was baptized at All Saints 23 July 1619, and Martha, 26 June 1621. Another daughter, Jane, was christened there 28 March 1623. A few months

[11]*Northamptonshire and Rutland Clergy*, IV, 107.

[12]*DNB*. According to this account he was born about 1549 and died 19 August 1645, making him age 96.

[13]Salter, *Oxford City Properties*, 127.

[14]Oxon. Archives, W.197.78; 70/2/23.

[15]*Northamptonshire and Rutland Clergy*, XV, 85.

later on 6 December 1623, Walter Wilkins died,[16] not yet forty years old, and the infant daughter, Jane, lived little more than ten years being buried 14 November 1633. Walter's widow married again, becoming the wife of the Reverend Francis Pope of All Saints, and was widowed again.

Jane Pope wrote her will 7 [or 9] day of June 1635, and it was proved a few days later on June 12 in the Court of the Chancellor of Oxford University. In it she appointed her father, John Dod, as her executor to distribute her estate among her children as he saw fit. In case he were unable or unwilling to serve, her brother, Timothy Dod, was named alternate. The inventory of her goods was made 17 June 1635 with Thomas Berry as one of the appraisers, and valued at £142/17/4 which included £100 for the lease of the house. Amongst the usual household goods was silver valued at £8. This consisted of two salts, one beer bowl, one beaker, twelve spoons, and one coral [child's silver-mounted coral teething ring or rattle]. In the stable was one silver girdle valued at 3s. 4d.[17]

John Wilkins, the eldest son of Walter and Jane Dod, became Warden of Wadham, a founder of the Royal Society, and Bishop of Chester. Their son, Timothy, was well known in his day as an epicure, a spendthrift, and a tavern friend of Anthony Wood. The third son, Peter, became a lawyer. Their talents probably derived from their mother's side of the family rather than from that of Walter Wilkins.

---

[16]Oxon. Archives, Endorsement of Walter Wilkins's Will.

[17]University Archives. There was another John Wilkins in Oxford in the first years of the 17th century. He was a locksmith who took two apprentices in 1605 and 1605/6, one whom was from Hook Norton. The relationship has not been established.

Will of John Wilkins, 1604, of Hook Norton, Oxon., father of Walter
Wilkins. Copyright Oxfordshire Archives. Reproduced with permission.

Samuel Wilkins

Samuel [sometimes spelled Samuell] Wilkins the second member of the family to engage in goldsmithing, was baptized at St. Peter's, Hook Norton, Oxfordshire, 18 June 1619, son of Thomas Wilkins and his wife, Alice, and nephew of Walter Wilkins, Oxford goldsmith. His father, a husbandman who died in 1628, left £20 to his eldest son, John, and £13/11/8 to Samuel, both bequests to be paid when the boys were twenty-one. Three servants were also named in the will, as well as cousins in Bloxham, Oxon.[1]

On 12 October 1632, Samuel was apprenticed to Thomas Berry of the City of Oxford, goldsmith, for a term of ten years.[2] He was admitted to the freedom of the City 4 December 1646.[3] His first apprentice was Alexander Wright, son of William Wright, gentleman of Oxford, who was enrolled 1 November 1649. Ten years later, 1 May 1659, Wilkins took another apprentice, William Robinson, son of Robert Robinson, gentleman of Oxford, but he was transferred to Daniel Porter, Sr. in 1668.[4]

By the time the Poll Tax was collected in 1667, he was living between 135 High Street and the Chequer Inn in All Saints parish. He paid a tax of 9s. for himself, wife, and seven children.[5] Only five of these children are accounted for in the All Saints registers: John, who became an Oxford goldsmith, baptized 23 August 1651; Mary, baptized 2 June 1655; Samuel, born 28 August 1656, destined to be an engraver in Warwick; Joanna, born 4 December 1659; and Martha, baptized 22 March 1661/2. Another daughter, Sarah, was named in his will as well as a son-in-law which implies that daughter was deceased. Samuel Wilkins paid 2s. in the Subsidy of 1667. In the Hearth Tax of 1665, he had paid

[1]Oxon. Archives, 70/3/13.
[2]Hanaster Book, 1613–1640, L.5.2.
[3]Hanaster Book, 1639–1662, L.5.3.
[4]*Ibid.*
[5]Salter, *Surveys and Tokens,* 227.

71

tax on four hearths, probably at 133 High Street in the Southeast Ward, All Saints parish.[6]

Samuel Wilkins's service to the city of Oxford was not extensive. On 30 September 1651, he was elected to the Common Council, and the following year he was elected chamberlain when it was noted that he compounded for a chamberlain's place for £6/13/4. He continued as a chamberlain, being elected every two years through 1664.[7] In 1688/9 his name appears in a list of chamberlains followed by the notation "mort."[8]

Neither is there an extensive record of work done by him. He began his employment at Wadham when his cousin, John Wilkins, was Warden of the college. In 1649 he was paid £5, and in 1656, 12s. Two years later he mended plate for £1/4/0.[9] In 1660 and 1661 he was paid 9s. and 12s. respectively for mending. It was ten years before he was employed again at Wadham and then it was for mending plate at 16s. 6d. From then to 1682 his work there was more constant with charges ranging from a pound to £3/18/6, all for mending.[10] A payment of £4/9/7 was made for unspecified work in 1686 to an unnamed goldsmith who was probably Wilkins. In 1689, 4s. was paid Wilkins on an old debt.[11]

Lincoln College paid him 6s. 2d. in 1658 for mending diverse plates.[12] At Corpus Christi College payments were made to Samuel Wilkins for mending, engraving, and changing plate from 1664 to the end of his life.[13] He did a bit of similar work at Balliol in 1667 and 1668.[14] Trinity paid him 17s. for a silver cup, probably for mending.[15] Anthony Wood, on 5 September 1670, paid him 11s. for a triangular silver seal engraved on one side with his coat-of-arms, with his crest on the second side, and the third side with his initials conjoined set within a wreath.[16] In 1676 he regilt the chapel plate at Brasenose for which he was paid £3.[17]

[6]Ibid.
[7]OCA, 1626–1665, 185 et passim.
[8]OCA, 1665–1701, 204.
[9]Wadham College MS. No. 22, 16/1.
[10]Ibid., 16/2.
[11]Ibid., 16/3.
[12]Lincoln College Calculus.
[13]Corpus Christi MSS. C/24/2 Box 1 and Libri Magni.
[14]Balliol College MS. Liber Bursarii, 1663–1677.
[15]Trinity College MS. Computi Bursariorum I A/3.
[16]Wood, Life, II, 202.
[17]Brasenose College Bursar's Book, 1663–1723.

There are only two references in the City records regarding Samuel Wilkins's occupation as a goldsmith. In 1660 he was one of the four men appointed regarding the replacement of the Great Mace which has already been discussed. Then in 1672/3 the City made payment of 11s. 6d. to him for a badge for William Prickett, cordwainer, who was a leather searcher in 1673.[18]

Most of his recorded employment was with the University. The Vice-Chancellor paid him 13s. 2d. for mending the bedels' staves several times between 1650 and 1652.[19] During 1653–1654 he engraved the University's arms on a stamp for books at the cost of £1. In the accounts for 1665–1666, payment of £1/1/3 was made to "ye Goldsmith for a silver Box in which was inserted ye Diploma of Colonel Strangewayes Degree, together with the Parchment and writing of it."[20] The goldsmith was probably Wilkins, and if so, he must have been also a calligrapher. A disbursement of 5s. was made in 1668–1669 to an unnamed goldsmith, who again was probably Wilkins, for mending the chains of the Vice-Chancellor's seal. Mr. Ball's staff was mended for 10s. by Samuel Wilkins during 1671–1672, and in the accounts of 1688–1689, 15s. was paid to "Mr. Wilkins" for mending the staff of "Mr. Colier ye Bedell." This staff also had been mended twenty years earlier.[21]

Wilkins made only one appearance before the Court of the London Goldsmiths' Company. On Wednesday, 10 November 1686, he was charged with selling a gold ring substandard. A fine of £4/6/0 was levied and he also was ordered to pay what the ring cost, then the ring was returned to him defaced.[22]

Samuel Wilkins signed his will with a very shaky signature 6 September 1688, declaring himself to be "of sound and perfect memory but considering the frailties and uncertainties of this mortall life," but making no mention of his occupation. He directed that his body be buried in the churchyard of All Saints. Bequests of 10s. apiece were made to his son-in-law, James Clarke and his wife, Sarah, Samuel's daughter; to his son, Samuel and his wife, Katherine; and to his son-in-law, Horatio Darling to

[18]OCA, 1665–1701, 327.

[19]University Archives, WPB/21/4, 276.

[20]University Archives, WPB/21/4, 285, 351.

[21]University Archives, WPB/21/5.

[22]Goldsmiths' Company Court Minute Book 9, p. 173. It is possible that this reference and the previous one regarding Mr. Collier's staff could have been to Samuel's son, John, who would have been free circa 1676.

buy them rings. Everything else, including ready money, plate of gold or silver, and jewels was to be divided equally between his dear and loving wife Elizabeth, and his son John Wilkins.[23]

Samuel Wilkins was buried 30 March 1689, age 69, and his wife followed him to the grave 19 May 1693.

[23]Oxon. Archives, W.204.128; 73/2/10. Neither Joanna nor Martha is named in the will. Martha may have been the wife of Horatio Darling, and Joanna is probably the "John, son of Samuel Wilkins" buried 16 December 1664, apparently mistakenly so written in the All Saints register.

John Wilkins the Elder

John Wilkins, known later in life as John Wilkins the Elder or John Wilkins, Sr., was baptized 23 August 1651 at All Saints, Oxford, the son of Samuel Wilkins, Oxford goldsmith, and his wife, Elizabeth. No record of his apprenticeship has been found, which would have occurred about 1666, and was probably to his father. Neither is there a record of his admission to the liberty of the City, but he would have been free by at least 1676. His only apprentice was his nephew, John Wilkins, enrolled in 1705.[1]

Wilkins's first work at Christ Church was in 1684–1685 when the college delivered to him twelve tankards to be melted and made into a like number of college pots. In 1697, the college ordered eighteen silver spoons, and twenty-four more in 1705. Also, between 1701 and 1705, he was engaged in changing plate for the college.[2] At Queen's in 1722 he engraved the branches of the chandelier in the college chapel.[3]

In 1692, he began working for Magdalen when he was paid £1/15/0. Five years later he was paid £1/10/0, but the following year, 1698, a payment of £37/0/0 was made to him. It is unfortunate that it is not recorded what this large sum purchased. From the beginning of the last quarter of the seventeenth century, Magdalen accounts consist of annual disbursements with no further notations. There are amounts ranging from only £1/2/0 to £5/7/0 about every two years except for £10/4/6 paid in 1708, £13/8/0 in 1724, and £22/6/0 the following year.[4]

At Corpus Christi many small payments were made to "ye Goldsmith," but rarely was the goldsmith's name entered. One bill for £2/8/0 paid 5 January 1709/10 was three years in arrears. Only once does John

---

[1]Malcolm Graham, ed., *Oxford City Apprentices, 1697–1800* (1987), #391.
[2]E. A. Jones, *Catalogue of the Plate of Christ Church, Oxford* (1939), Introduction, xi.
[3]W. G. Hiscock, *A Christ Church Miscellany* (1946), 136.
[4]Magdalen College MSS. LCE32 and LCE33.

Wilkins's name appear. He was paid £5/11/6 "for changing plate, etc." 29 October 1713.[5] His employment at Balliol was sporadic, being only in 1709, 1710, 1715 and 1722.[6] As might be expected, the Wilkins tradition continued at Wadham. In 1698 he was paid £2/8/0 for mending college plate, and £2/13/0 in 1705.[7] Some earlier payments to "Mr. Wilkins" could have been to him or to his father.[8]

John Wilkins's work for the University was more consistent. In the Vice-Chancellor's Accounts for 9 October 1706 to 9 October 1707, a payment was made to him of £1/17/6.[9] In 1710–1711, he mended the Bedel's staff for £1/0/0, then Mr. Thistlethwayte's staff needed mending in 1713–1714, at a cost of 11s. 6d. for this and a medal, but a goldsmith's name is not entered; however, it likely would have been Wilkins. During 1711–1712, 10s. had been paid to an unnamed goldsmith for "mending the Beedles staffs." Wilkins was paid 5s. in 1717–1718, and £1/7/0 the following year.[10]

There are two items of special interest in the Vice-Chancellor's Accounts. The first one is, "Item paid Mr. Wilkins the Goldsmith per bill £177/4/6, October 7, 1722–October 7, 1723." The next year (1723–1724), is "Item paid Mr. Wilkins the Goldsmith per bill £91/19/6."[11] After repeated mendings of the old staves the University apparently decided it was time to purchase new ones. Accordingly, six were ordered from Benjamin Pyne, a leading London goldsmith who was a prolific maker of municipal maces and regalia. Three are silver-gilt and three are silver, all of the same design except that the silver ones are slightly smaller. All bear full London hallmarks and were made in 1723–1724. It was customary for orders for plate from London goldsmiths to be placed through an Oxford goldsmith who probably offered advice on which London goldsmith was best for the purpose at hand. The Oxford goldsmith then did the engraving of arms and inscriptions. The charge of £177/4/6 would have been for the gilt staves, and the £91/19/6 for the silver ones. These charges would have included Wilkins's engraving

---

[5]Corpus Christi Libri Magni c/1/1/15.
[6]Balliol College Liber Bursarii.
[7]Wadham College MSS. 16/3 and 16/4.
[8]These are detailed under Samuel Wilkins.
[9]University Archives, WPB/21/6.
[10]*Ibid.*
[11]*Ibid.*

of the coat-of-arms on the flat top of each stave.[12] These staves are still in use.

In the Vice-Chancellor's Accounts for the year 1694–1695, £2/0/0 was paid to the Marshal for a badge.[13] Presumably he was being reimbursed for the payment made to a goldsmith who was probably John Wilkins as his father, Samuel, had done the University's work until the end of his life and John Wilkins is the only goldsmith mentioned in the accounts until the end of his life. The University Church of St. Mary the Virgin has deposited the badge in the Ashmolean Museum. It bears no hallmarks nor maker's mark and is rather crudely made, all adding to the supposition that it was of local workmanship. The University arms with scrolls above are repoussé. The book in the arms if quite angular and the motto, *Dominus illuminatio mea* is not properly spaced thus coming up short at the end. The oval badge, measuring 12.5 cm. × 16.4 cm. and weighing approximately 6 oz. 3 dwt., has a flange with the holes punched all around for sewing it to the sleeve of a gown.

John Wilkins was a vestryman of All Saints for many years beginning in 1695 and continuing for most years until 1710. In 1711, the parish paid him 2s. for mending the great silver flagon which with its cover weighed 56 oz. 12 dwt., and in 1713, they paid him 6s. for changing a plate.[14]

Wilkins did not escape the attention of the London Goldsmiths' Company. On Thursday, 8 August 1706, "Mr. Wilkins of Oxford appeared by Mr. Lofthouse and submitted for selling Gold wares worse than standard." He was ordered to pay £1/5/6 the cost of the goods plus £1/2/0 fine.[15] His second and last brush with the Company occurred on Thursday, 3 September 1719, when he appeared before the Court in person for selling gold and silver wares worse than standard. He paid a fine of £7/18/6 which included the price of the goods.[16]

Like other members of his family before him he held offices in the City government. Beginning in 1701, he was repeatedly elected bailiff until

---

[12]*Vide* Moffatt, *Old Oxford Plate* (1906) for a complete description of the staves. Unlike mace, "stave" denotes authority, in this case, the authority of the University.

[13]University Archives, WPB/21/5.

[14]Oxon. Archives, D.D. Par. Oxford. All Saints a.1 (1607–1716).

[15]Goldsmiths' Company Court Minute Book 10, p. 313a. Seth Lofthouse, London goldsmith; mark entered as a largeworker in 1699; dead by 1727.

[16]Court Minute Book 12, p. 9.

1717 and in that year he was elected keykeeper as well.[17] Wilkins was elected 12 September 1719 as one of the eight assistants in place of Richard Broadwater who recently had died, but he asked to be excused from accepting this and any office in the future because of his infirmity and lameness. For this privilege he offered to pay a fine of £25.[18] Perhaps the dampness of the Thames Valley had a deleterious effect on him. Although he lived another eight years, this statement of his infirmity raises the question of whether it was he or his nephew and namesake who was responsible for the University's work during those years, including the procurement of the new staves.

John Wilkins never married and he apparently continued to reside in the family home. The property at 135 High Street was described as twenty feet wide. The south portion, the backside of the Guildhall, was listed as being occupied by John Wilkins from 1718 onwards,[19] but he must have been there, if not from the time of his birth, at least from his early childhood. He apparently held other property as 8 October 1720, he took out a policy with Sun Fire Insurance Company on a house only in the parish of All Saints, Oxford, described as "late in the Tenure of George Hopkins now Empty."[20]

Being of sound health and good and perfect mind, he wrote his will 2 January 1716/7, naming his niece, Mary Clarke, to receive £1000, and specifying that she was to continue to live with his executor [her cousin] "for one whole year gratis without any thing for Meat drink Washing or lodging during the time aforesaid." Mary's sister, Elizabeth Clarke, his niece, received £20, and his nephew, Samuel Wilkins, got 20s. Mary Putty, his servant, was bequeathed "twenty guineas in case she shall continue Servt. to the time of my decease." All the residue of his estate, John Wilkins left to his nephew, John Wilkins who had been his apprentice and journeyman, and who was named his sole executor.[21]

John Wilkins the Elder died on Sunday, 7 January 1727/8, aged 77, and was buried in the evening of 9 January in All Saints Church. Thomas Hearne wrote that "he was very rich, being always a single man," as though his bachelorhood was the cause of his wealth. Hearne went on to

[17]OCA, 1701–1752, 2 et passim.
[18]Ibid., 115.
[19]Salter, Survey of Oxford, I, 170.
[20]London Guildhall Library, MS. 11936/12, 242.
[21]Oxon. Archives, W.94.176; 157/2/42.

repeat gossip he had heard that Wilkins had left £1000 to Mr. George Cooper, the University Registrar, whose second wife was related to Wilkins with whom she had lived for a number of years. He was supposed to have promised her £1000 to be paid at his death upon her marriage to Cooper. Again to quote Hearne, "The rest Mr. Wilkins hath left (being, said, three or four thousand libs.) to a nephew that lived with him."[22]

Oxford was a small enough city, even in the early eighteenth century, for tongues to wag. In comparing Hearne's remarks with Wilkins's will it is obvious the gossips were not well informed—they seldom are. It is unfortunate no inventory exists for any member of the Wilkins family, except Jane Wilkins Pope, but it appears their fortunes increased with each generation.

---

[22]*Remarks and Collections of Thomas Hearne,* IX, 389–391.

John Wilkins II

The Wilkins star continued to rise with John Wilkins II, the nephew of John Wilkins the Elder who when his uncle died in 1727/8 was left a fortune on which to build. Apprenticed to his uncle 27 August 1705, for a term of seven years, he was the son of Samuel Wilkins, engraver, late of Warwick,[1] and his wife, Katherine. He was probably born in Warwick circa 1690, and would have gained his freedom, of which there is no record, about 1712.

John Wilkins the Younger no doubt worked as a journeyman for his uncle, but with his death he came into his own. By 1730 his name began to appear in college accounts and those of the University. Beginning in the seventeenth century, Brasenose kept all the actual bills of all tradesmen who did any work for the college, hence a marvelous picture is preserved of the dealings of John Wilkins with the college. It also shows something of how Brasenose handled its finances—very casually. It sometimes took three or four years for bills to be paid.

There was nothing casual, however, about Wilkins's bills. They were extremely detailed with everything strictly itemized in a large, clear, easy-to-read hand. As a result, it can be determined what he actually made, the cost per ounce of the silver, the cost for making, gilding, and engraving, as well as the allowance he made for old silver, calculated by the ounce, that the college turned in against payment. When the cost for making is not stated, it can be assumed that he was retailing the piece which he had obtained from a London goldsmith.

During 1730 he mended and engraved plate and made some. A polished punch bowl weighing 52 oz. 8 dwt. at 7s. 6d. per ounce was billed at £19/13/0. Engraving it was 12s. 6d. The polished punch ladle weighing 2:8:12 cost 14s. 7d. for the silver plus 7s. 6d. for making it as well as 2s. for an ebony handle, plus 3s. for engraving the college arms. With the

---

[1]Graham, *Oxford City Apprentices, 1697–1800*, #391.

cost for *making* the punch ladle listed separately and not for the punch bowl it is probable that he was retailing the bowl from a London gold-smith. Toward this bill the college turned in Sir Ralph Ashton's plate weighing 74 oz. 10 dwt. at 5s. 2d. per ounce making a credit of £19/5/0, leaving £5/10/7 owed by the college. Ashton was probably the donor of this silver now headed for the melting pot.

On February 1, 1731, he billed the college for two polished castors, the gift of Mr. Lindley, weighing 17 oz. 11 dwt. at 8s. equalling £7/0/5; two salts costing £2/0/4½ plus 14s. for making. Engraving the college arms and gentleman's arms on each piece cost £1/8/0. A mustard spoon at 4s. 6d. brought the total to £11/7/3½.

From 15 January to 11 August 1732, Wilkins's bill of £36/13/0 was mostly for mending and engraving, but also included two decanters weighing 60 oz. 18 dwt. at 7s. 2d. totalling £21/16/6 plus £1/10/0 for en-graving three coats-of-arms and two inscriptions on each one. Toward this bill, on 21 December 1732 he took in four old tankards weighing 84 oz. 1 dwt. at 5s. 2d. yielding £21/14/3. He also had received a bit of silver on 13 September valued at 3d. This bill was finally paid 30 November 1733.

Wilkins did a large amount of mending and engraving costing £9/16/0 between 17 December 1733 and 6 December 1737. Toward this the col-lege turned in old plate worth 19s. 5d. On 8 December he was paid the balance. During 1736–1737, he engraved four tumblers with the college arms and inscriptions at a cost of 12s. 6d. He made four cauldron salts; the charge for making them was 9s. 6d. each, and engraving each was 7s. On this bill he took in five old hafts, four old forks, four old salvers and three tankards for a total of £18/3/6 leaving a balance of 19s. 5d. in favour of the college.

The year 1746 was a busy one for Wilkins. His account with Brasenose included polishing an old square candlestick and fixing a false socket in it. His labour was 7s. 6d. plus 3s. 6d. for 12 dwt. worth of silver added. He made a pair of double-jointed snuffers and a snuff pan engraved with the college arms and inscriptions, six cauldron salts with the usual engraving, salt shovels, and teaspoons. The college also ordered a new candlestick to match the old square one on which he then engraved the college arms and an inscription on it and one on the old candlestick. Twelve old tankards with a total value of £50/3/7, two small tankards and a pair of candlesticks, snuffers and pan, a branch for candles, and two salts, all valued at £31/5/4 were turned in for credit. After three bills the account for 1746 was finally paid by the Reverend Mr. Davie, bursar, on 28 December 1749.

1737   Brasen-nose College Debtors to J. Wilkins for

                                                 £ S S

Dec: 10:th   mending Mr Farrington's Plate — — — 0 : 4 : 0

           Mr Walthalls plate — — — — — 0 : 3 : 6

   14   graving ye College arms and Coll: Æn: Nas. on 4 Candlesticks — — — — } 0 : 11 : 0

Feb: 7:th   mending Mr Thellwals plate — — — 0 : 5 : 0

Mar: 29:   Mr Lysters plate — — — — — 0 : 3 : 6

           Mr Litchfields plate — — — — 0 : 3 : 0

June 14:   Mr Kents plate — — — — — 0 : 5 : 0

   29   Mr Barkhams Salver — — — — — 0 : 0 : 6

   30   Graving a pollished Tankard with Two Coats and an Inscription ye gift of Mr } — 0 : 12 : 6 Howard — — — — — —

Nov: 9:   Beating out and cleaning ye Mr Howards Plate — — — — — — } 0 : 01 : 0

   17   mending Mr Lindleys Caster — — — 0 : 01 : 0

                                Totall   2 : 10 : 0

Nov: 30: 1738 Recd of ye Revd Mr Parr Bursar the Contents in full for worke done for the College &c pr John Wilkins

Bill of John Wilkins. Brasenose College Archives.

In the Brasenose archives is a letter from Richard Green "goldsmith opposite Durham Yard in the Strand," dated London, June 20, 1738, to the bursar:

> I rec'd a letter from Mr. Stonehouse of ye 14th with Orders to send to your College a Tankard of about Eight or Nine pounds Value for Mr. Howard which I have sent this Evening to the Coach, the Tankard I have sent is in the Newest fashion & comes to more than my Orders please to let the Gentm. see it & if he approves of it I shall take an opportunity to draw on you for the mony [*sic*] which is Ten pounds ten shillings.
>
> A Tankard wt. 28 oz. 10 dwt.
> @7s. 4d. per oz.   £10.9.−
> Box etc.   1
>   £10.10.0
> Directed for Mr. Howard to yr. Care

John Wilkins's bill for 1737–1738 included the engraving of this polished tankard with two coats-of-arms (presumably those of the college and the donor) and an inscription "ye gift of Mr. Howard." The cost was 12s. 6d. Wilkins's total bill for the year was £2/10/0, and the college managed to pay it without the usual delay, being receipted on 30 November 1738.

In 1754 among the usual mending and engraving, Wilkins charged 9d. for engraving an inscription on a Dutch chafing dish. He also obtained a red leather case for the Grace Cup at a cost of 14s.[2]

St. John's College began employing John Wilkins in 1730 when he was paid £23/16/0. In 1735 he mended Mr. Morley's tankard for 4s. This tankard appears in the 1662 inventory, indicating it would have been given by Morley then or at some earlier date. Wilkins also did mending, boiling, and burnishing, and made several salts. Old silver valued at £8/17/8 was turned in leaving £19/5/1½ due out of £28/2/9½. On 15 June 1737 Katherine Wilkins (his wife) signed that she had received "the full contents of this Bill."

The amount of work varied greatly from year to year; for instance, in 1741, he was paid £2/17/0, and in 1749, £20/13/8, in which year he made a polished cream boat and teaspoons, and engraved six half-pint mugs. Such work for St. John's continued to the end of his life.[3]

---

[2]Brasenose Archives, Tradesmen's Bills are bundled according to trade and year.
[3]St. John's College Subsidiary Accounts ACC<u>V</u>.B.1.

New College employed him in 1732–1733 to do repairs, engraving, to make spoons, and to gild a basin weighing 200 oz. 2 dwt. At 2s. per ounce, the cost was £20/0/1. His total bill came to £51/8/11½ which was partially offset by Wither's old tankard weighing 68 oz. 8 dwt. worth £17/11/4. It was replaced by a new tankard of 74 oz. 12 dwt. which at 6s. 11d. per ounce cost £25/15/10½, and then Wilkins charged 16s. for engraving it with two coats-of-arms and an inscription.[4] Wither was probably the original donor, and the new tankard would have had the same engraving as the old one which was customary in all the colleges as well as with the City's plate.

In 1729 Wilkins was paid 3s. for engraving a pint cup plate at Jesus College, but further transactions lack details. In 1743 was entered, "Mr. Wilkins, the silversmiths Bill £9/0/11," and in the following three years his bills were for only a few shillings each.[5]

As could be expected larger amounts were paid to him at Wadham: In 1736, £10/12/10; 1746, £10/17/2; and 1752, £17/12/10, but there are no descriptions of the work done.[6] He began working for Corpus Christi in 1736 and continued until 1754 when he was paid £19/2/7 with the largest payment being £28/3/0 in 1737.[7] At other colleges such as Balliol, Oriel, Christ Church, Magdalen, and Queens he was active in doing repairs, engraving, and probably making salts.[8]

Payments ranging from a few shillings to a few pounds were made to Wilkins by Pembroke during the twenty years 1736 to 1756.[9] On 19 August 1732, however, he had been paid £29/15/6 for a gilt basin and for engraving it. The basin was for use in the college chapel,[10] as an alms dish. Measuring 16 1/8 inches in diameter, it bore the London hallmarks for 1731–1732 and the maker's mark of Edward Pocock. The beautiful engraving of the arms of the college and the arms of Benjamin and Nicholas Hyett, brothers who matriculated from Pembroke in 1724 and 1725 respectively, and the Latin inscription stating it to be their gift, all surrounded by scroll mantling, decorated the depressed centre of the

[4]New College 1154.
[5]Jesus College Buttery Accounts.
[6]Wadham College 16/4.
[7]Corpus Christi College c/1/1/16.
[8]Bursars' Books of the relevant colleges.
[9]Pembroke College 4.3.4 and 4.3.5.
[10]Ibid., A.1.1.

otherwise plain gilt basin.[11] The engraving was the work of John Wilkins.

All Saints parish where Wilkins was a vestryman in 1728, 1732, 1739, and 1745, paid him a shilling for marking a plate and a pot in 1735, and five years later, 3s. with no reason given.[12] He did no work for any other Oxford parish; but of course, the churches had little use for a goldsmith, except perhaps for soldering a leaking chalice on rare occasions.

John Wilkins II followed his uncle as the University's goldsmith and continued as such until the end of his life. He, in turn, was followed by his former journeyman, Edward Lock. The first payment to Wilkins was in 1732–1733 for £13/16/6 on the University's Account. Since there had been no payment to a goldsmith since the purchase of the new staves nine years previously, this sum may have included arrearages.[13]

Minuscule amounts were paid for cleaning and mending until "Boxes for the Diplomat, etc." were purchased for £4/15/6 in 1736–1737. The following year Wilkins's bill was £3/1/6. This latter amount may have been for the Marshal's baton which like the old staves has silver wrapped around a wood core. The top end has the University arms in a shield in repoussé. The other end is engraved "Oxon. Univ. 1738." The baton bears no assay nor maker's marks. It is very probably the work of John Wilkins II.

Payments continued to be made to him ranging from a few shillings to a few pounds, the largest amount being £4/4/6 in 1754–1755. The next and last payment the University made to him was in 1757–1758 in the sum of £1/11/6 for a silver box and for cleaning the "Beadles Staff."[14]

E. A. Jones attributed the great number of salts of the eighteenth century which survive in Oxford colleges to John Wilkins. They bear full London hallmarks and a maker's mark, I·W a mullet above and a rosette below in a circle. In an inventory of University College plate compiled by H. Clifford Smith in 1943, four salts of 1765 and two of 1771 are attributed to Wilkins who died in 1757. Jones explains his attribution with the suggestion that George Tonge, his late apprentice

---

[11]Moffatt, *Old Oxford Plate* (1906), 195 and Plate XCV. The college no longer possesses this piece.

[12]Oxon. Archives, D.D. Par. Oxford, All Saints, c.4 (1721–1752).

[13]University Archives WPB/21/6.

[14]University Archives WPB/22/1.

and journeyman, continued to use the mark for the benefit of Mrs. Wilkins. He, however, apparently was not aware that Mrs. Wilkins quit business in 1759, moved to Bath and died in 1764. There would have been no reason for Tonge to continue the use of the mark as late as 1771 when he was so well established in his own business. The maker was more apt to have been a London goldsmith who evidently specialized in salts. Grimwade suggests the mark may belong to a member of the Wood family.

It appears that it was customary for Oxford goldsmiths to act as intermediaries for the recovery of stolen plate. It was advertised in *Jackson's Oxford Journal* 4 April 1756, that a silver candlestick was stolen from the Marquis of Tichborne at Christ Church. A reward was offered to the person returning it to Wilkins, goldsmith. There are numerous advertisements of this sort in the newspaper.

John Wilkins played a distinguished rôle in the government of the City of Oxford. On 30 September 1728, he was chosen Mayor's child, and being present, took the oath and paid 3s. 4d. for not being constable. A year later he was chamberlain and in 1730, keykeeper. The next year he was junior bailiff. There was a ceremony in connection with authority being transferred to newly elected officials. In the Council Acts of 29 September 1732 it is described thus:

> The late bailiffs, Mr. John Wilkins and Mr. Thomas Munday, then bring in the City treasure, £57.10s., to which they each added 5s. making £58, and the new bailiffs pay £5 and £13.6s.8d. and are sworn, and the late senior bailiff delivers the keys of the City gates to the new senior bailiff, and the late junior bailiff delivers the City treasure, £58, and a leather purse to the new junior bailiff. The new bailiffs are then sworn.[15]

In 1733 Wilkins was bailiff, and the following year was elected one of the eight assistants in the place of one who was deceased. He took the usual oaths and paid £5 and £8. A month later he was chosen Mayor, an office he again held in 1744. In 1737 he was elected alderman. Until the end of his life he was an assistant, dying in office.[16]

John Wilkins died 22 December 1757, and *Jackson's Oxford Journal* reported in the issue of Saturday, December 24, 1757: "Last Thursday died here after a lingering illness, Mr. John Wilkins, an eminent Gold-

---

[15]*OCA, 1701–1752*, 165 *et passim.*
[16]*Ibid.*, 189 *et passim*, and *OCA, 1752–1801*, 1 *et passim.*

smith of this City, who had twice served the Office of Mayor, and was a senior assistant in this Corporation."

Calling to mind the gilding of a 200 oz. basin at New College in 1732–1733, one wonders if he did much gilding that does not appear in extant records. At that time gilt was applied by making an amalgam of gold and mercury then rubbing this paste onto the surface to be gilded. When the object was fired the mercury was vaporized leaving the gold attached to the surface of the silver. Mercury fumes are deadly poison and when the work is done repeatedly in a room which may not have proper ventilation, it can be very detrimental to health. This could have been the cause of his lingering illness.

Wilkins had three apprentices. The first was Stephen Hedges, son of William Hedges of Iffley, Oxfordshire, mason, apprenticed for a term of seven years from 21 February 1734 at the time Wilkins was Mayor. Nothing more is known of him. George Tonge, son of Henry Tonge of Oxford, fisherman, was apprenticed to him 26 May 1746 for seven years,[17] and Edward Lock, son of Edward Lock of Bicester, but there is no record of his apprenticeship. Both continued to work as journeymen for Wilkins until his death and then for his widow until she quit business in May of 1759. Mrs. Wilkins apparently was a partner of her husband in the business as she is referred to in college accounts as Katherine [or Catherine] Wilkins, Goldsmith. She died at Bath in mid-January 1764.[18]

Six months after John Wilkins the Elder had died, his nephew, John Wilkins, had petitioned the City to allow him to make a doorway into the Town Hall yard where there had formerly been a door. June 28, 1728, the City agreed to it and he was required to pay 15s. per annum for the privilege and to provide two locks and keys, one of which was to be left with the City "to prevent entrance through the same when they think fit."[19]

The business continued in the High Street until it was closed by Mrs. Wilkins, but in 1740 they had changed their residence to 36 Castle Street in the parish of St. Peter-le-Bailey. On 10 May that year a lease was granted by the City to John Wilkins for 30–36 Castle Street for a rent of 2s. and two capons. It was four tenements with the drawbridge to the east. There was a separate lease for No. 36, granted the same day describing it

[17]Graham, *op. cit.*, #1586 and #1901.
[18]*Jackson's Oxford Journal,* January 15, 1764.
[19]*OCA, 1701–1752,* 163–164.

as a tenement now in Wilkins's occupation, formerly occupied by John Carter. The rent was 6s. 8d. and two capons with a fine of £12.[20]

A son was baptized 6 November 1736, noted in the All Saints register as "John, son of John and Catherine Wilkins." He matriculated in the University from Worcester College 22 November 1753, age 17; received his B.A., 1757 and M.A., 1760. He is listed in the matriculation register as "son of John, of Oxford (City), gent."[21] Nothing more is known of him.

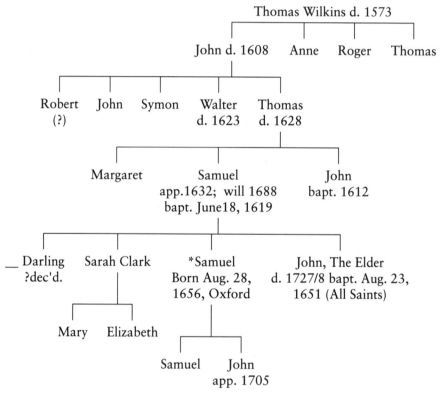

* Engraver of Warwick. His wife was Katherine. Probably the Samuel Wilkins who was buried at All Saints, Oxford, on January 16, 1696.

[20]Salter, *Oxford City Properties*, 226.
[21]Foster, *Alumni Oxoniensis*.

George Tonge

George Tonge, son of Henry Tonge of Oxford, fisherman, and Hannah Vincent Tonge, was baptized at All Saints, Oxford, March 13, 1729/30.[1] He was apprenticed to John Wilkins, goldsmith, for seven years, being enrolled May 26, 1746.[2] Following the completion of his apprenticeship he remained as a journeyman with John and Catherine Wilkins until she quit business in 1759, eighteen months after her husband's death.

At the beginning of June 1759, he opened his own shop near the Bear Inn in the High Street where he promised a "good Assortment of the neatest, and most fashionable Plate of all Sorts." He assured his prospective customers that he "executes all the various branches of the Business, in the neatest Manner," and that he "makes Mourning, and other Rings, etc. and gives the most Money for Old Gold and Silver."[3]

It was only natural that the colleges which had employed John Wilkins would favour George Tonge with their custom following the retirement of Wilkins. He had assisted in handling the business for Mrs. Wilkins following her husband's death. During that first year, 1758, he collected £1/19/0 from Brasenose for beating, cleaning and mending in the name of Mrs. Catherine Wilkins. When he was established in his own business he did mending for the college in the succeeding two years, and engraving in 1762.[4]

In that same year University College paid him 9s., presumably for repairs.[5] He did similar work at Oriel between 1761 and 1768, in 1781, and between 1770 and 1780, but in 1769 he was paid £13/10/8 for Sir Anthony Cope's cup weighing 50 oz. 15 dwt. which was charged at 5s. 4d.

[1]There is another baptismal entry in the parish register dated April 3, 1730.
[2]*Graham, Oxford City Apprentices, 1697–1800,* #1901.
[3]*Jackson's Oxford Journal,* June 2, 1759.
[4]Brasenose College, Hurst, 70–75.
[5]University College Bursars' Accounts.

per ounce.[6] During most of the years between 1761 and 1780, he was doing work for Balliol,[7] and at Corpus Christi between 1765 and 1769 he was paid sums ranging from 9s. to £14/9/0.[8]

Between Michaelmas 1761 and Michaelmas 1762, Pembroke College paid George Tonge £2/0/0 for unspecified work, once again following in the footsteps of John Wilkins. Three years later he was paid 13s., and in 1771–1772, 10s. for mending plate, and the following year, £2/2/0 for mending and altering plate. During the succeeding two years there are entries in the Bursar's Book for new blades to knives with payment made to Tonge. This undoubtedly referred to Richard Tonge, George Tonge's brother who was a cutler.[9]

In 1760 Tonge began working for Magdalen College. Four years later he was paid £24/8/2, but between 1774 and 1779, payments ranged from £1/2/0 to £5/3/3.[10] No description of the work done is given. The only work he seems to have done for Lincoln College was in 1775 for 9s. 5d.[11] The sums were much larger at Trinity College where in 1775 he was paid £24/2/2 and in 1777 £36/1/0, but in the year in between he received only £5/4/0. His employment there continued every year to 1793.[12]

It was at St. John's College that George Tonge really came into his own. December 26, 1759, he was paid £1/12/6, of which 15s. 6d. was due Mrs. Wilkins. December 20, 1760, he collected 16s. which included 10s. for "mending and boiling ye silverwork & silver added to the Crosier July 14." May 20, 1763, Tonge received from the college a large cup and cover weighing 140 oz. which he gilt inside and out at 2s. per ounce equalling £14/0/0. Mending the cup and cover cost 3s. 6d. and a new leather case for the same was £1/4/0. The total bill of £15/7/6 was paid June 4, 1763. December 4, 1769, he supplied a mahogany knife case with French plate furniture for £2/8/0, and in 1770, he did various bits of mending amounting to £2/18/6. Between January 13 and October 10, 1773, there are forty-five entries in the Bursar's Books for mending, cleaning, engraving and making two salt ladles and a mustard spoon, totalling £7/6/5.[13]

[6]Oriel College Treasurers' Accounts, 1.E.17.
[7]Balliol College Computi Bursarii.
[8]Corpus Christi College Libri Magni.
[9]Pembroke College 4.3.6.
[10]Magdalen College Bursar's Records.
[11]Lincoln College Calculus.
[12]Trinity College Computi Bursariorium I A/5; I A/7.
[13]St. John's College Subsiduary Accounts ACCⅩ.B.1.

Between 1773 and 1781 George Tonge had many transactions with St. John's. To be regretted now is the fact that the college disposed of much old plate in the process as witnessed by the following accounts retained in their archives: Six tankards and three cups of various donors are listed. Then, Mr. Bentley's Pint, Six Tumblers. Mr. Hart's, Mr. Roberts's, Mr. Orlebar's, and Mr. Benson's spoons totalling 246 oz. were valued at £65/19/0. Tonge signed a receipt for this stating, "Rec'd Feb. 5, 1773 of the President ye above plate which I Promise to be accountable for." Added to this list were the following: "A Crewett Stand & Casters from £23 to aney Price. A case of Knives forks & spoons about £31/10/0. A Dish Stand from £9/9/0 to 12 or 14 guineas. Mr. Medleys 3 & 6 halfpint 15 oz. at 5s. 4d. £4/0/0. 1773."

Ten of these same objects in the list as well as the spoons appear in an inventory of 1662, with the weights the same as in 1773. One of the tankards weighed 34 oz. 17 dwt., and two small ones each weighed 12 oz. 19 dwt.

In Tonge's billing certain items are listed as having been made by him while others, probably the work of London goldsmiths, he retailed but engraved. Charges for the making and for the silver used is separate. Examples follow:

> Feb. 2, 1776—making four Cup't Saltes £3/0/0.
>   Sterling at 23 oz. 9dwt. at 8s. per ounce £9/7/8.
> Sept. 20, 1777—A pollished Chas'd Tea Urn
>   Wt 106 oz. 6 dwt. at 9s. per ounce £47/16/8
>   Heater & Key 3s. 6d.
>   Engraving ye Arms & Inscript on ye Urn 14s.
> Nov. 4, 1777—Making two pollish'd Chas'd Tea Vazes £6/10/0
>   Sterling wt. 27 oz. 10 dwt. @ 5s. 10d. per ounce £8/0/6.
>   Engraving ye Arms & Inscript: on Ditto 18s.
>   Making Three Hand Candlesticks £4/14/6.
>   Snuffers 9s.
>   Sterling Wt. 28 oz. 11 dwt. @ 5s. 10d. per ounce £8/6/6.
>   Engraving ye Arms & Inscript: on Ditto £1/11/6.
> Jan. 29, 1780—Making three pairs of Beaded Oval Salts £4/1/0.
>   Glasses 6s.
>   Sterling Wt. 22 oz. 7 dwt. at 5s. 6d. per ounce £6/3/0.
>   Engraving ye Crest & Inscript: on each 10s. 6d.

Other pieces made were knife hafts, table spoons, a pair of butter ladles, gravy spoons, and forks. Items purchased from him included sauce boats, waiters, a bread basket, a dish stand, and a mahogany case with silver furniture.

The bill through March 27, 1779 amounted to £257/14/10. The old silver received on February 5, 1773 [listed here as received on February 4] was applied toward the bill. On September 20, 1777, twelve plates weighing a total of 203 oz. 10 dwt. @ 5s. 8d. per ounce equalling £57/13/2, and three plates weighing 51 oz. 7 dwt. @ 5s. 8d. per ounce equalling £14/11/10 were taken in against the bill. March 3, 1778, he received a draft from the college president of £40, and on April 20, 1778, he received an old bowl weighing 66 oz. 4 dwt. @ 5s. 6d. per ounce equalling £18/4/1. All this totalled £200/7/3. Other purchases were made May 8, 1779, raising the total indebtness to £272/18/4. December 9, 1779, the bill was finally paid in full. It appears that he required the old silver to be deposited with him before he started work or made purchases.

From January 29, 1780 to October 6, 1780, Tonge's bill amounted to £156/17/3. On March 23, 1780, he received Teynham's Punch Bowl weighing 102 oz. 15 dwt. @ 5s. 6d. per ounce equaling £28/5/1. By December 10, 1781, the remainder of the bill had been paid in cash.[14] The college must have run out of a supply of old silver.

George Tonge's civic career began in 1762 when he was elected to the Common Council to fill up the place vacated by Edmund Ayshcomb who had resigned. He and others, after being sworn, promised to pay £3/10/0 in lieu of entertainment and 3s. 4d. for not being constables. In 1764 he was again chosen for the Council and the following year he and John Wyatt purchased chamberlains' places at the price of £6/6/8, and he continued in this office until 1770 when he became junior bailiff. Tonge progressed through the offices of bailiff and keykeeper and assistant to September 17, 1781, when he became Mayor. Two years later he was again an assistant, and on March 17, 1783, he was elected an alderman in the place of Phillip Ward, deceased. After being sworn he paid £10/0/0 for entertainment. In 1800 he was still an alderman; and at times, keykeeper as well.[15]

One wonders how he found time to carry on the business of goldsmithing. Besides holding offices in city government, he served on various committees. September 20, 1784, Tonge, by now termed "Esquire," was elected one of the Barge Commissioners, and on November 11, he and six others constituted a committee to consult with another committee ap-

[14]Ibid.
[15]OCA, 1752–1800, 51 et passim.

pointed by the county justices to consider the selling or leasing of the room and ground under the Grand Jury room as a place for the clerk of the peace to deposit the county books, papers and records. The committee was to make its report at the next Council. The following year he was a member of a committee of five appointed to attend the next meeting of the commissioners of the Thames Navigation of Oxford to inform them of the damages done to the City estates on the river by the tenant of Woolvercott [Wolvercote] Mills in penning the water at King's Wear [Weir].[16] In 1788 he became Justice of the Peace.[17] April 5, 1798 he resigned as a member of the Market Committee, and also as Commissioner of Sewers and Barges. A few days later he was appointed to represent the City in a meeting with a representative of the Queen's College to settle differences concerning the limit of the lands in a City tenement and one owned by Queen's.[18]

At his business premises George Tonge acted as an agent for lost and/or stolen silver, jewellery and watches. A number of advertisements appeared in the *Oxford Journal* listing such items and stating that enquiries should be made to Mr. Tonge, goldsmith. A notice appeared in the March 3, 1778 issue of the *Journal* that Elizabeth Lay of Fifield had brought a silver chalice cover to Tonge, apparently in an effort to sell it to him. As it was supposed stolen, she was imprisoned. He also acted as collector of debts for Peter Rowbotham, a mercer in the Cornmarket who was selling off his stock.[19]

The General Provident Society was established in 1787, and Tonge was one of the two treasurers,[20] and in the same year he was taking subscriptions for the newly established Sunday schools.[21] In December 1775, the Reverend John Cox, L.L.D., of St. Giles bought a lottery ticket from George Tonge and won £5000. The lucky clergyman shared his good fortune with the prisoners in the Castle.[22] Along with all these activities he carried on the fishing tackle business of his late brother, Richard, fishing tackle maker and cutler whose house had been near All Saints Church.[23]

[16]*Ibid.*, 161 *et passim.*
[17]*Jackson's Oxford Journal*, July 26, 1788.
[18]*OCA, 1752–1801,* 258.
[19]*Oxford Journal*, January 1, 1785.
[20]*Ibid.*, March 20, 1787.
[21]*Ibid.*, January 31, 1787.
[22]*Ibid.*, December 7, 1775.
[23]*Ibid.*, October 2, 1782.

He also found time for two apprentices. The first one was Richard Hickman, son of Edward Hickman of Great Missenden, Buckinghamshire, yeoman, enrolled 11 December 1766 for a seven-year apprenticeship.[24] His second apprentice was Thomas Turner, son of Elizabeth Turner, who was enrolled 25 February 1774 on payment of £60.[25] In the first instance Tonge is spoken of as "goldsmith," but in the latter he is referred to as "silversmith."

According to the *Oxford Journal* of May 11, 1763, George Tonge married the eldest daughter of Mr. Madge of Chilton, Buckinghamshire, near Thame. Following a long illness she died at Chilton in June 1781, and a year later, 10 June 1782, he married Ann, widow of Richard Madge, Oxford grocer, at Chilton. Tonge was living in Chilton, and the bride was of the High Street in All Saints parish, Oxford.[26]

George Tonge had his shop along the High Street façade of the site of the Covered Market which opened in 1774, and adjoining it was the shop of his brother Richard who died in 1782.[27] July 1, 1774, the City gave a lease to the Mayor and Aldermen of a garden occupied by George Tonge bordering to the north a garden of Brasenose College with the Guildhall Court to the west. This must have been the location of the property which he had insured 7 February 1780. It is described as his dwelling house in All Saints, timber and slated, for a sum not exceeding £200. His utensils and stock, plate included, was insured for a sum not exceeding £2800, making for a total of £3000. In this policy with the Sun Fire Insurance Company he is described as silversmith and toyman.[28]

By 1802 George Tonge was no longer living in Oxford although he was an alderman of the City. He was listed in the 1802 Poll Book of Oxford as a resident of North Hinksey, Berkshire, and he was buried there in the parish of St. Lawrence September 3, 1802. *Jackson's Oxford Journal* in its edition of Saturday, August 28, 1802, noted: "Yesterday morning died, in the 73rd year of his age George Tonge, Esq. Senior Alderman and

[24]Graham, *op. cit.*, #2332.

[25]*Ibid.*, #2492.

[26]*Oxford Journal*, June 6, 1781; June 10, 1782; Bishop's Transcript and Marriage License, Buckinghamshire Record Office, Aylesbury. There is no record there of his first marriage. There must have been a relationship between his two wives; it is possible that his first wife was a sister of his second wife's first husband.

[27]Salter, *Oxford City Properties*, 376; Green and Roberson, *Studies in Oxford History* (1901), 334.

[28]London Guildhall 11936/281, 376.

Father of this City." September 11, the *Journal* recorded the fact that Edward Lock, Esq., goldsmith and banker and Senior Assistant of the Corporation was unanimously elected one of the aldermen to fill the place of George Tonge, Esq., deceased. It was rather like an old boys' network even in death.

Tonge had signed his will November 30, 1793, leaving all his "ready money, securities for money, Goods, Chattels, real and personal estate and effects of whatever nature" to his dear wife, Ann, after the payment of his few debts and funeral expenses. His wife was named executrix in the will which was probated in the Prerogative Court of Canterbury.[29]

In spite of this will, there is a strange document in Oxfordshire probate records dated April 12, 1826, nearly twenty-four years after his death. He had departed this life without having surrendered or assigned the remainder of a term of five hundred years on property in Kidlington, and no legal personal representative of him could be found. Tonge had acquired the property by indenture of mortgage 6 July 1771, with the mortgage paid off 9 August 1792. It consisted of "that capital Messuage or Tenement with the houses outhouses buildings gardens orchards close commons and appurtenances thereunto belonging then formerly in the tenure and occupation of James Almont his undertenant or undertenants . . . all of which premises were situate lying and being in the town parish and Fields of Kidlington alias Cudlington in the County of Oxford."

Henry Albert Mayberry was appointed administrator, and it was decided that Ann Pulley of Weston-on-the-Green, Oxon., widow, and Thomas Pulley of the same place, yeoman, were entitled to the freehold and inheritance of the property.[30] Not a clue is given as to why the Pulleys should be the heirs, or why nearly a quarter of a century was allowed to elapse before a claim was made. George Tonge's personal life remains shrouded in mystery.

---

[29]P.R.O., P.C.C. Will, Prob. 11/784.

[30]Oxfordshire Archives, Bd. Appt. of Proxy. 288/1/23; 306/13/6, Oxford Consistory and Archdeaconry Probate Records 1733–1858 and Oxfordshire Peculiar Probate Records 1550–1858.

Edward Lock I

Members of the Lock family played a significant rôle in the life of Oxford from approximately the mid-eighteenth century well into the succeeding century. Three generations of them were goldsmiths and it is sometimes difficult to distinguish one from another as college and University records tend to state only the surname.

First of the name to appear in Oxford was Edward Lock. He was the son of Edward Lock and was baptized August 20, 1730 at St. Edburgh, Bicester, Oxfordshire in which parish an Edward Locke, son of Nycholis Locke, was christened September 6, 1641. No apprenticeship record exists for Edward Lock, goldsmith, but other evidence indicates that he was apprenticed to John Wilkins the Younger, probably about 1745, and remained with him as a journeyman.

The year 1759 marked important changes in Edward Lock's life. February 22 he was admitted to the liberty of the City upon payment of 20 guineas and official fees.[1] He obviously knew that Mrs. Wilkins soon would be retiring and it would be necessary for him to set up shop on his own. He accordingly advertised in *Jackson's Oxford Journal* May 26, 1759, that since Mrs. Wilkins had retired he was intending to carry on business in the High Street across from his former place of employment. Then on June 14, he was married at All Saints to Hannah Bridge of Bicester. Edward Lock was 29, and his bride 24.[2]

Lock was soon prospering which is not surprising as he and George Tonge were now sharing the lucrative trade which had been achieved by John Wilkins. Following the death of Mrs. Wilkins, he became the lessee of Wilkins's former property in the parish of St. Peter-le-Bailey on May 2, 1764. This was located at No. 30–33 Castle Street and consisted of four tenements occupied by William Vasey, Thomas Davey, Margaret Wheeler, spinster, and Catherine Hanmore, spinster. Lock also obtained the lease

[1] *OCA, 1752–1801,* 34.
[2] Oxon. Archives, Oxf. dioc. papers d.63f. 12.

of No. 36 Castle Street, which had been the last Wilkins residence, but then occupied by Jane Woodward, widow.[3]

On February 10, 1767, Lock took out a policy with the Sun Fire Insurance Company in which he is described as silversmith and hardwareman. Insured for a sum not exceeding £100 was his dwelling house of brick and timber and tiled situated in the High Street, Oxford. Obviously he was conducting his business from the same premises as the utensils and stock therein were insured for £200, and the plate therein for £350. Also included in the policy were two tenements in the parish of St. Peter-le-Bailey, timber and slated, one in the tenure of William Vasey, shoemaker, and Thomas Davy, breechesmaker, not to exceed £30. The two spinster tenants apparently had moved out or died, but Jane Woodward was still occupying the tenement at No. 36 Castle Street. That was insured for £20.[4] June 27, 1771, the policy was renewed for the same total of £700, but then the four tenements were occupied. Davey and Vasey were still there and there was one Cole. The fourth tenant was Joseph Lock.[5] This may have been Joseph Lock, malster.

The first work Lock did on his own seems to have been at Jesus College when he was paid 8s. in 1759. He continued to work for them through 1793 with the biggest entry being that year for £23/10/6. This could have been for work done by his son, Joseph. Most of the payments ranged from a few shillings to a few pounds, but in 1762 he was paid £19/9/11 for exchanging of plate, and £1/11/9 for mending. This is the only specific notation in the Jesus records.

The personal account of James Matthews, the college bursar, records payment of £8/4/0 October 28, 1773, for a silver coffee pot. There is no way of knowing if Lock made the pot or was simply retailing it. The following January 3, Mr. Matthews purchased a pair of silver buckles for 16s. with 7s. 6d. being allowed for the old ones. On June 4, 1776, Matthews notes that he had paid Mr. Lock, goldsmith, but with no further information.[6]

Lincoln College made payments to Lock of £2/0/7 for work done between 1763 and 1767, and £4/9/0 for 1764–1765. Only 1s. 6d. was paid him in 1775, and £1/16/9 in 1784. He continued to be employed by the

[3]Salter, *Oxford City Properties,* 226.
[4]London Guildhall 11936/173, 592.
[5]London Guildhall 11936/207, 294–295.
[6]Jesus College Buttery Accounts.

college and in 1794–1795 it was noted that the college had received from him in the fourth quarter interest of £25 on £500.[7]

In 1774 and 1778, mending of plate was done for Brasenose,[8] and a little work was done for Pembroke. In 1779–1780 Lock received 3s. for mending; three years later £1/1/10, and the following year 11s. 9d.[9] At Balliol he was employed consistently from 1775 through 1797,[10] and at Oriel beginning in 1772.[11] It was only natural that Edward Lock would be chosen goldsmith at Wadham after the demise of John Wilkins. Here it is especially unfortunate that the records are not detailed as large payments were made to him following his first employment there when he was paid five guineas April 22, 1765. Among smaller payments, which would have been for mending, in various years, the sum of £15/17/6 was paid April 27, 1769. In 1781, his bill was £32/6/11, and in 1786, £61/9/6. These latter two were large expenditures, but there is no itemized account.[12]

The University, like most of the colleges, employed one goldsmith throughout his lifetime; hence, Edward Lock followed Wilkins here also, being paid £4/1/0 for three silver boxes in 1759–1760. He and his son Joseph continued to supply these boxes well into the nineteenth century. Some were known as skippet or seal boxes, while others were used to hold addresses to various personages. For instance, in 1789–1790, the University paid £5/5/0 to Lock and Son for two gilt boxes for addresses of congratulations to their Majesties the previous year on the King's recovery. They were also used for the presentation of diplomas to such as the High Steward.[13]

It is unlikely that these were actually made by Lock, but rather were probably supplied by Richard Goldwire of St. Clement's parish, at least in the second half of the eighteenth century, and then retailed to the University by Lock who possibly did the engraving on them. Eric Delieb in his *Silver Boxes* pictures two of them engraved with the arms of the University and dated as mid-Georgian by the style of engraving. They bear the single mark RG which Delieb assumed to be the maker's mark of a

---

[7]Lincoln College Calculus 1660 ———.
[8]Brasenose College, Hurst, Tradesmen's Bills.
[9]Pembroke College 4.3.6.
[10]Balliol College Computi Bursarii.
[11]Oriel College Treasurer's Accounts ETC B2.
[12]Wadham College 16/5.
[13]University Archives, WPB/22/1 and WPB/22/2.

London goldsmith, but which he had not identified.[14] The University bought dozens of these boxes over the years and on one occasion, in 1771–1772, Lock was paid £30/3/0 for an unspecified number of them. Although known a century earlier, they did not seem to come into fashion until 1736–1737 when Wilkins was paid for "Boxes for the Diplomat."[15] Lock's only other work for the University consisted of cleaning the Marshal's Badge for 4s. and "for cleaning and new gilding the Beadles' Staves etc." at a cost of £26/13/0 in 1772–1773.[16]

Lock took three apprentices. The first was Thomas Jackson, May 27, 1767, then his son Joseph, April 18, 1774, and finally John Davis, October 3, 1785. Further details of them are given elsewhere.

Edward Lock frequently appeared in the pages of *Jackson's Oxford Journal*. On more than one occasion there is mention of watches bearing his name as maker, but it is possible that he only was retailing them as there is no other indication he was a watchmaker. He may have made the cases. There were attempts by various felons to sell him stolen goods but he was adept at getting them prosecuted. One Lucy Bennett (formerly Smith), the daughter of a Worcester College butler, brought him a silver spoon which she wished to sell. It was known to be part of a large quantity of plate stolen from the college. It was reported January 18, 1769 that she was taken before a magistrate and allowed bail until the Assizes at which she was convicted and transported for seven years. Another person who in 1772 attempted to sell him a stolen spoon was a little luckier, succeeding in an escape from the constable. A vivid description is given in the *Oxford Journal* of another criminal episode which occurred in 1784:

> Ann, wife of Richard Edwards, was committed to Oxford Castle by Mr. Edward Lock, charged on the oath of Henry Parrott of Salford, on violent suspicion of stealing over 18 Pounds in gold and silver on the morning of 5 September from Henry Parrott. 7½ guineas were found concealed in the cushion of her headdress and a 2s 6d piece in the lining of her stays. To accomplish the robbery she had prevailed on Parrott (then in liquor) to cohabit with her the preceding night. Her husband Richard Edwards and George Cox were also about this time committed to the Castle for stealing horses and a prisoner's clothes, in Witney Bridewell.

In 1788 some more thieves were committed to prison by Lock.

[14]Eric Delieb, *Silver Boxes* (1968), 20–21.
[15]University Archives WPB/22/1.
[16]University Archives WPB/22/2.

Numerous notices appear in the *Journal* for property to let with inquiries to be made to Edward Lock, goldsmith. When John Wood, described as man-midwife, died in the summer of 1764, Lock had his house in Pennyfarthing Street to let. In 1767 he had a tenement in Pennyfarthing Street available which was then occupied by the Miss Forresters. Eleven years later Joshua Platt, retired supervisor in Oxford and collector of fossils, died, and Lock was advertising to let his house in Pennyfarthing Street. This may have been the same property each time and again in 1784. He also had a stone house next to the Lamb in St. Giles in 1765, and in 1774, a farm at Charlton-on-Otmoor which was in the possession of Absalom Kirby.

Edward Lock took a very active part in City government and various civic endeavours. His political career began September 29, 1762 when he was named chamberlain. The following year he was nominated as Mayor's child and promised to pay 3s. 4d. for not being constable. He served variously as bailiff, keykeeper and assistant until he was elected Mayor in 1776, and paid £15 when sworn. Following his term he continued to hold City offices at least through 1800.[17]

Lock was appointed June 3, 1771 to a committee to determine the value of the City interest in its houses, buildings and grounds within the City and its liberties, as the City was looking toward the sale of these properties. This committee was also charged with pulling down the Bocardo at the City's expense, but it was specified that the old materials and the ground were to be reserved for the City's use.[18]

There was little in the life of Oxford with which Edward Lock was not concerned. Transportation was becoming of paramount importance with the need for coal to be moved more quickly and thus more economically from the Midlands coalfields to Oxford. Great enthusiasm was aroused for the construction of a canal beginning in Coventry which would join the Thames. In 1768 a promotional meeting was held in Banbury at which £50,000 was immediately subscribed.[19] The following year the City became heavily involved in the project with the formation of the Oxford Canal Company, but it was not a concept that could be brought to fruition quickly. Seven years later the *Oxford Journal* reported in its issue of May 29, 1776 that a meeting of the Oxford Canal Company was convened by Edward Lock and fifteen others at the Star to dis-

---

[17]*OCA, 1752–1801*, 51 *et passim*.
[18]*Ibid.*, 88–89.
[19]Jessup, *A History of Oxfordshire*, 95.

cuss the proposed junction of the Oxford and Coventry Canals. In 1784 he was a member of the Company of Proprietors of the Oxford Canal Navigation.[20] The canal which proved to be very profitable, was not completed until 1790.

In that year Lock and Son were agents in Oxford of the Banbury Five Years' Tontine Society.[21] This was a type of an annuity insurance group. In the meantime Edward Lock was appointed, in 1774, receiver of gold coins as designated by an Act for calling them in. Two years later he was mentioned as a changer of deficient gold coins.[22]

Banking was to become the cornerstone for the family's increasing wealth. In 1788 the New Oxford Provident Society was established with Lock and Son as treasurers. Then some two and a half years later it was announced that a bank connected with Childs Bank in London was to be opened in Oxford by Thomas Walker, Esq., and Company. William Jackson, Joseph Brooks and Edward Lock and Son were his partners, and business was to be carried on in the latter's shop until possession of the adjoining house could be obtained.[23] This was evidently the messuage known as the Three Black Potts or Black Potts Alehouse on the north side of High Street next to Edward Lock's property on the west. When the City sold the fee simple for £140 to Lock in 1787 it was occupied by James Radford, victualler. The property had been willed to the City in 1713 by Charles Harris of Oxford, gentleman, reserving the income from it to his wife for her lifetime, then to his son Charles Harris for his life, and then to his daughter Elizabeth for her life. Following the death of the last heir the City was to use the rent-money for bread to be distributed to the widows and children of poor freemen on Easter Eve.

The Mileways Act of 1771 put an end to this charity as the Commissioners decided that part of the house should be razed to widen the street with the remainder sold to Lock.[24] The money thus obtained by the sale was invested for the benefit of the Oxford Turnpike.[25] So much for charity. Charles Harris, gentleman, the benefactor, was the son-in-law of Alderman William Wright, goldsmith.[26] Harris also bequeathed 100 ounces

[20]*Jackson's Oxford Journal,* January 14, 1784.
[21]*Ibid.,* August 21, 1790.
[22]*Ibid.,* July 16, 1774; April 27, 1776.
[23]*Ibid.,* February 5, 1788; September 4, 1790.
[24]Salter, *Oxford City Properties,* 140–141.
[25]*OCA, 1752–1801,* xxviii.
[26]Wood, *Survey of the Antiquities of the City of Oxford* (1899 ed.), III, 168.

of plate to the City.[27] Amends, however, already had been made in advance by the City Fathers as in January 1784 a meeting was held at the Town Hall at which J. Watson, Mayor, and Edward Lock were appointed treasurers to distribute bread to the industrious poor every Sunday and Wednesday morning.[28]

Jackson's Oxford Journal reported in the issue of April 15, 1787 that Mrs. Lock, wife of Edward Lock, goldsmith, of Oxford died after some years of ill health. Hannah, age 53, was buried at All Saints four days later. Edward lived on for another twenty-six years, dying at the age of 83. He was buried at All Saints September 14, 1813.

[27]OCA, 1752–1801, 79.
[28]*Jackson's Oxford Journal*, January 30, 1784.

Joseph Lock

Joseph, the only son of Edward and Hannah Lock, was baptized April 17, 1760 at All Saints, and was apprenticed to his father for seven years April 18, 1774,[1] and was admitted free in 1782.[2] Upon the completion of his apprenticeship he continued to work with his father as various accounts show. The Plate Book of Oriel College contains an invoice from Edward Lock & Son in 1782 for salt ladles, an argylle, and a pair of candlesticks.[3] Beginning in 1785, the Vice-Chancellor's Accounts sometime specify payments being made to Mr. Lock & Son.[4] Oriel made payment to Lock in 1806,[5] but there is no way of knowing which one was actually responsible for the work. It is likely, however, that much of the business was retailing.

Beginning in 1786, Joseph Lock took his place in City Government as chamberlain and was admitted the Mayor's child. He was re-elected chamberlain in 1788, 1790 and 1792. In 1792 he was authorized by the City along with four others to vote for the City at the next or special meeting of the Oxford Canal Navigation to be held at Banbury. Lock continued to hold City posts, being named senior bailiff and keykeeper in 1793. From 1794 through at least 1802 he continued as bailiff.[6]

The number of poverty stricken people in both the County and City of Oxford had been increasing through the last quarter of the eighteenth century, and by 1800 the situation reached alarming proportions. More than a third of the City's population was being aided.[7] December 24, 1799, the Council decreed that 100 guineas were to be paid by the City Treasurer "for the relief of the poor inhabitants of the City." A subscription for this "laudable purpose" was opened to which the members

[1]Graham, *Oxford City Apprentices, 1697–1800,* #2497.
[2]E. A. Jones, Catalogue of the Plate of Oriel College, Oxford (1944), addendum, xxi.
[3]Oriel College sIIG26.
[4]University Archives, WPB/22/2.
[5]Oriel College ETC B2.
[6]*OCA, 1752–1801,* 175 *et passim.*
[7]Jessup, *A History of Oxfordshire,* 103-105.

present very generously contributed from their own pockets. On the same day a general meeting of the inhabitants of Oxford was held to consider the situation of the poor and to contribute funds for their relief. Joseph Lock was one of the committee to carry out the general purpose which had been proposed.[8]

In view of such praiseworthy activities, one might suppose that Joseph Lock was dearly loved by the populace. The reality of the matter was quite the opposite, at least as far as the inhabitants of Headington Quarry were concerned. The enclosure award of 1801 gave him extensive lands at Headington among which was an old footpath from Quarry to Headington which was the means of carrying coffins to the parish church. By 1805 Lock had built a wall across it. With the next funeral the participants demolished the wall and Lock rebuilt it. Like a childish spat this episode was repeated, and he took three of the participants to court.

James Palmer, the curate of Headington, wrote to the Bishop of Oxford venting his opinions of Mr. Whorwood, the lay rector, Whorwood's brother the vicar, and Joseph Lock. Regarding the last named, he wrote:

> Mr. Lock, whose improper conduct has made no inconsiderable disturbance in this parish, is a person in whose estimation the possession of money is a compensation for the absence of almost everything else, and although Mr. Whorwood *to my certain knowledge* most heartily despises him, yet he finds it convenient to show him some civilities and attentions, for it is said that he has borrowed money of him. Mr. Lock would not be so much disliked as he is, if he did not permit his wife, who is a busy, meddling woman, to interfere as much as she does in everything in which he is concerned. He suffers her to make a fool of him, therefore he is a fool.[9]

Lock attempted to enlist Palmer's help in his court proceedings, but he did not get it. In his letter to the Bishop Palmer explained the situation regarding it as an insult to the Church. He added:

> I am not to be dazzled by any man's wealth, and can very clearly see the dangerous tendency of that blind adoration paid to riches, which is so prevalent at the present time. The injury complained of originated from an undue respect to the wealthy citizen's money bags.[10]

[8]*OCA, 1752–1801,* 272–273.

[9]Oxfordshire Archives, Oxf Dioc pp c657.

[10]*Ibid. Vide* Carl Boardman, *Oxfordshire Sinners and Villians* (1994), 52–54 for a full account of the affair.

This meddlesome wife was Elizabeth Watson, daughter of Sarah and of Benjamin Watson, Oxford grocer who was deceased when Joseph Lock married her May 1, 1781 at St. Peter-in-the East.[11] At the age of 62, she died October 25, 1822 according to the inscription on the monument to the Lock family which was erected in All Saints Church, but according to the parish register she was not buried until December 31. Seven children died between 1788 and 1806, but a son, Edward, baptized at All Saints April 25, 1785,[12] survived to be apprenticed to his father for seven years being enrolled April 24, 1799.[13] He, however, is beyond the scope of this work.

The Lock family fortunes had continued to increase with Joseph as banking became more important and lucrative than the goldsmithing craft. Different references to him describe him as "banker and goldsmith." When he died January 16, 1844, age 84, he was Sir Joseph Lock, Knight. Nine days later he was buried at All Saints.[14]

Joseph Lock's will proved in the Prerogative Court of Canterbury March 29, 1844[15] illustrates how far the family had come in two generations from their origins in Bicester. The twelve-page complicated will with provisions for trusts, signed January 8, 1844, shows him to have been something of a Renaissance man with wide-ranging interests. Having already buried his wife and seven children his only direct heirs were his daughter Maria, the wife of George Baker Ballachey, his son Edward and Edward's children, Edward Seppings Lock and Helen Seppings Frances Lock, both of whom were minors. The sum of £100 was left to his kinsman, Joseph Lock "now or late in the Office of Messieurs Mayhew Solicitors Carey Street London." Perhaps he was a grandson of Joseph Lock of the City of Oxford, malster, whose son was a London goldsmith.

Joseph Lock was possessed of extensive lands in the parishes of All Saints and St. Clement, in the enclosure of grounds known as the Northern Meadows in the parish of St. Giles, lands in the parish of Iffley adjoining the London Turnpike Road which he had "purchased at the time of the Iffley Inclosure with all the buildings and appurtenances," other freehold messuages within the city and suburbs of the City of Oxford and in the parish of Headington, as well as copyhold lands and hereditaments at Headington. He maintained homes in both Oxford and Headington.

[11]Oxfordshire Archives, Oxf. dioc. papers d.63f. 360; *Jackson's Oxford Journal*.
[12]Oxfordshire Archives, Top. Oxon. c.172.
[13]Graham, *op. cit.*, #3161.
[14]Oxon. Archives, Top. Oxon. c.172.
[15]P.R.O., P.C.C. Will, Prob. 11/1995.

Detailed provisions were made for carrying on the banking business in which his partners were his sons and William Taylor. One share in the Oxford Canal Navigation was willed to his daughter, noting that it had belonged to her mother and had come to him at her death, and one share in the Oxford Gas Light and Coke Company. More interesting and illustrative of the tastes of Joseph Lock are the enumerations of the contents of his homes and other chattels.

To his daughter he bequeathed all the household furniture and articles of household including linen and china in his house at Headington with the exception of such things as his son may have purchased and sent there while he was resident there. Maria was also willed everything else at Headington which included the greenhouse and all the plants therein, all the horticultural and agricultural implements, three garden engines and the water cart, cattle and all livestock, his coach, phaeton and old chariot together with the carriage horses and harnesses, the cart horse bought from Mr. Whorwood, the chestnut nag, the pony, donkey and three carts and the pony carriage and two ponies given to Sir Joseph by Captain Wilson.

The contents of the house at Oxford also went to Maria. Even the housekeeping provisions, wines, liquors and other consumables are mentioned as well as the furniture and fixtures in her bedchamber and adjoining closet along with all the pictures and drawings therein. Also in this bequest was the oil portrait of Dr. Crotch and seven framed cartoon prints. Maria received her father's diamond cluster ring and his single stone diamond ring, and all the following items: Ivory Crucifix and stand, grand pianoforte, organ, harp and Spanish guitar, all his music books and music in manuscript. One wonders if Sir Joseph had tried his hand at musical composition. Edward received the violoncello and kettle drums.

Art as well as music apparently was an important part of life in the Lock family. Maria inherited a frame of miniatures, paintings, drawings, figures, busts, vases, flowers, casts and medals, some of which may have been executed by her. She was also given two marble busts, other busts and figures, reliefs of silver, copper, iron, lead, sulphur, plaster, wax or other compositions, coins, medals and medallions, along with all cabinets, chests, drawers, glass cases, and boxes which housed the collection.

Maria must have had an interest in science as well as in art and music as her father bequeathed her his globes, telescope, glass machine for drawing shadows, a solar microscope, two concave mirrors, and all his optical, philosophical, electrical, magnetical, or chemical machines and apparatus, a glass blowing machine and rosewood work table and teapoy. There was also a mineral collection, fossils, shells, coral, ores and stalactites.

Appended to the will is a schedule of the plate bequeathed to Maria listed in Part 1, and to Edward in Part 2. Of the seventy-two lots weighing a total of 774 ounces in Part 1, there was a considerable amount of flatware. Larger pieces included a teapot, 27 oz. 9 dwt.; kettle, stand and lamp, 58 oz.; coffee pot, 29 oz.; cream jug, 7 oz. 15 dwt., and a sugar vase and cover, 11 oz. 16 dwt. All these were chased with flowers, and a tea caddy weighing 12 oz. 19 dwt. was chased with flowers and a shell. A tall cream ewer with square foot weighed 2 oz. 15 dwt., and a cream pail with blue glass liner, 3 oz. 6 dwt. An oval waiter weighed 34 oz. 4 dwt., and among candlesticks were a tall pair with square feet, 32 oz. 10 dwt. A chased tankard weighed 13 oz. and a chased cup with a handle for beer, 5 oz. 12 dwt. There were six cheese patties totalling 7 oz. 21 dwt. and a gilt casket, 15 oz. 13 dwt. Two sauce tureens were listed at 48 oz. and a bread basket at 28 oz.

Edward received plate with a total weight of 783 oz. 7 dwt. This begins with a melon-shape teapot weighing 25 oz. 10 dwt. and a tea urn, 115 oz. 6 dwt. followed by a coffee urn with a ram's head, 30 oz. 4 dwt. A soup tureen with plates and ladle weighed 147 oz. 14 dwt.; a hash dish, stand and lamp, 59 oz. 4 dwt., and a round tea waiter, 41 oz. 3 dwt. Among fifty-three lots were a siphon weighing 11 oz. 13 dwt. and five plain teaspoons and one other "lately found at Headington" totaling 2 oz. 18 dwt. Edward also received six cheese patties of the same weight as those Maria received. A chased wine strainer and stand weighed 7 oz. 1 dwt.; a plain cream jug on a round foot 2 oz. 17 dwt., and a plain cup with a handle, 4 oz. 17 dwt. Among other items was the usual array of flatware.

It is unfortunate that there is no indication if any of this plate came from the Lock workshop or from that of John Wilkins II when Joseph Lock's father, Edward, was a journeyman there. The tall square footed candlesticks were likely to have been eighteenth century. The cream pail with the blue glass liner was most certainly circa 1770, and the several pieces of flowerchased tea and coffee wares were probably eighteenth century rococo. The melon-shaped teapot could have been circa 1735 or an early nineteenth century revival of the style, and the round-based cream jug and square-based cream ewer eighteenth century, the latter circa 1790.

Edward Lock laid the foundations of the family banking business and thus of the family fortune. Joseph Lock expanded his interests far beyond the craft of goldsmithing and even banking. It was banking, however, which provided the means of acquiring lands, art and other accoutrements of the so-called good life.

Makers' marks of Oxford goldsmiths present a real problem since there was not a guild in the city. E. A. Jones tentatively attributed the mark J·L in a rectangular punch with clipped corners, which appears on a considerable number of pieces owned by Oxford colleges, to Joseph Lock, son of Edward Lock. These items all bear full London hallmarks ranging in date from 1776 to 1818.[16] Since he was not apprenticed until 1774, this obviously is not his mark. Rather, it belongs to Joseph Lock, son of Joseph Lock of the City of Oxford, malster, who was apprenticed under the London Company to John Moore June 6, 1764 on payment of £20. He entered this mark as a smallworker May 26, 1775, and spent his working life in London.[17] It is quite possible that some of the entries in college records of payment to "Mr. Lock" or "Lock the goldsmith" refer to this Joseph Lock.

At Trinity College, however, there is a curious cylindrical mug which may be the work of Joseph, son of Edward Lock. It is of a form which harks back to Queen Anne with earlier Stuart features with sharply sloping sides and wide reeded bands at the top and bottom. The S-shaped handle ends with a heart-shaped spur. It is engraved with the college arms in a rococo cartouche of mid-eighteenth century style above which is TRIN: COLL: OXON:. Below the armorials is an inscription, *Hoc poculum ignotae vestustatis d.d. Henricus Georgius Woods Præses* [This cup of unknown age was given by Henry George Woods, President] and the date 1894.

Trinity's Benefactors' Book throws no great amount of light on the problem. The President's gift is recorded as being "a hooped Pint Pot of silver, supposed to be the work of the silversmith who made the Dilke Tankard which is in the College's possession." That is attributed to either Joshua Lejeune or John Lautier, and is hallmarked London, 1785.

There are several problems with this attribution. Neither of these goldsmiths is listed in Grimwade. Both are listed in Jackson (Pickford edition) as registering their marks in 1773, but a mark is shown only for John Lautier and that is I·L in a rectangular punch with clipped corners. On the bottom of the mug is a maker's mark IL in an oval punch stamped four times in the manner of London hallmarks, and no other marks. A mark very similar to this is shown in Grimwade as belonging to John Lefebure, a London

[16]Jones, op. cit., addendum, xxi; 33-35; 43.

[17]A. G. Grimwade, London Goldsmiths, 1697–1837 (1982), 584.

Mug possibly by Joseph Lock, and the maker's mark on the bottom. Courtesy of the President and Fellows of Trinity College, Oxford.

goldsmith who registered his mark as a smallworker in 1720. In this mark, however, there is more space between the edge of the letters and the surrounding oval. Although this date seems to coincide better with the style of the mug, there is the problem of only a maker's mark stamped four times and the total absence of London hallmarks. Many times if an object was not "set for sale;" i.e., made to special order, it was not sent for assay.

The style of the armorials is later than the style of the mug, and both are earlier than the working life of Joseph Lock. The question remains — did Joseph Lock copy a mug, including the engraving of Trinity's arms, for the college, and how did it come into the hands of President Woods at the end of the nineteenth century?

It should be noted here that most Trinity plate bears an extra mark, CT in a rectangular punch. Moffatt assumed that when repairs were made to various items the goldsmith doing the work stamped his mark on them.[18] Actually, the mark stands for *Collegio Trinitatis*. An eighteenth century inventory of college plate contains a note of clarification written by Dr. Joseph Davie, Fellow of Trinity and in 1778–1779 the college bursar. The note at the beginning of the inventory dated 1778 reads, ". . . N.B. The letter 'M' is affixed to such pieces of Plate as have the weight stamped on them: And those 'P.S' to such as have the Private Stamp of C.T. on them."[19]

Joseph Lock's father, Edward, did register his mark, E·L in a rectangular punch, with the London Company July 30, 1762,[20] but Joseph did not. It seems rather strange that the Oxford colleges should have by-passed the local Lock goldsmiths in favour of another son of Oxford working in London. It is quite possible, though, that his work was being retailed by his probable relatives in Oxford.

There were others of the name in the city. Edward Lock and Sarah Door, both lodgers in St. Peter-le-Bailey, were married September 18, 1786, and Joseph Lock and Mary Higgins, widow, of Marcham, Berkshire, were married October 2, 1766 at St. Giles.[21]

---

[18]Moffatt, *Old Oxford Plate,* 160–165.
[19]Trinity College MS. Silver Plate, Plate 2.
[20]Grimwade, *op. cit.,* 240.
[21]Oxon. Archives, Oxford City Marriage Licenses.

William Wright I

The Wright family truly could be called a dynasty of goldsmiths, flourishing from the last quarter of the sixteenth century to beyond the first quarter of the eighteenth century. During these approximately 150 years only three Christian names were borne by the goldsmiths in the family; i.e., William, Martin and Alexander, in a complicated web of relationships.

The first of them, William Wright, son of Robert Wright of the City of Oxford, tailor, was apprenticed to Thomas Gower, goldsmith, February 11, 1575/6, and received his freedom by *copia patris* November 14, 1586.[1] The date of his apprenticeship would place his birth at circa 1560-1561. The family probably was domiciled in Oxford for many years. A William Wright, tailor, appears in the rent rolls of Oseney Abbey as residing in the parish of St. Mary Magdalen in 1459.[2] In 1481 a Robert Wright held a lease in the parish of St. Michael Southgate, and another Robert Wright "once of Henry VIII College" had the tenure of a garden in Catte Street in 38 Henry VIII [1547].[3] It is impossible to say, however, what the connection was, if any, with the goldsmithing Wrights. William Wryght and Robert Wryght were living in the Southeast Ward, probably at 77 High Street and 86-87 High Street respectively at the time of the Subsidies of 1543 and 1544. This Robert Wryght, who had goods worth £5,[4] may have been the father of William Wright, goldsmith, whose wife was Joane Winter.[5]

---

[1]Hanaster Book, 1514-1591, A.5.3.

[2]Salter, *Cartulary of Oseney Abbey* (1931), III, 266.

[3]Salter, *Survey of Oxford*, II, 35; I, 80.

[4]Salter, *Surveys and Tokens*, 143.

[5]Wood, *Survey of the Antiquities of the City of Oxford*, III, 166. In his *Life*, II, 12, he mistakenly refers to her as Katherine.

111

William Wright was simultaneously a goldsmith and a baker, a very odd combination of trades, and an alderman as well. The trade of baking may have been in the family as a William Wryght, apprentice of Roger Holden, brown baker, gained his freedom in 1551/2.[6] This may have been the William Wright buried at St. Martin's June 7, 1596. There appears, however, to be no extant apprenticeship record for William Wright, goldsmith, as a whitebaker, but in 1615, 1618, 1621 and 1631, the last about four years before his death, he took apprentices as such.[7] October 5, 1615, he was admitted whitebaker to the University, and on October 12, 1620, the Vice-Chancellor ordered the bakers and butchers to set up their stalls in the market. John Wright, whitebaker, was matriculated November 30, 1637.[8] This may have been a son of William, but there is no baptismal nor apprenticeship record for him. Circa 1610–1620, William Wright is mentioned as one of the common bakers of the town and suburbs. They ground corn at the Castle Mill owned by the City.[9] In 1636, Balliol made payment to Martin Wright, William's son, on behalf of his father for supplying bread to the college.[10]

As though all this were not enough to keep him busy, he took several apprentices as a goldsmith. The first one recorded was George Cary in 1589, then Thomas Crompton in 1594. The next one entered was Thomas Wyse in 1607, followed by Thomas Greene in 1617.[11] The freedom of two other of his apprentices is recorded in the *Oxford Council Acts*: Walter Wilkins and Martin Wright, his son, although there is no record of their apprenticeships in the Hanaster Books. Furthermore, Wright carried on an active trade as a goldsmith. One suspects that a great deal of the actual work of both baking and goldsmithing was accomplished by the apprentices, some of whom may have remained as journeymen.

The first known instance of Wright's employment as a goldsmith was at Christ Church in 1584, and he continued to do work for the College until 1616. March 29, 1598, he was paid for a livery pot weighing 15¼ ounces which was charged at 5s. 6d. per ounce, and 18d. for engraving the names of the donors, making a total of £4/5/4.[12] Eighteenth century

[6]W. H. Turner, *Selections from the Records of the City of Oxford,* 1509–1583, 212.
[7]Hanaster Book, 1613–1640, L.5.2.
[8]Andrew Clark, *Reg. of the Univ. of Oxford,* Part I, Introduction, 338-339.
[9]*OCA, 1583–1626,* lxi.
[10]Balliol College Liber Bursarii, 1615–1662.
[11]Hanaster Books, 1514–1591, A.5.3; 1590–1614, L.5.1; 1613–1640, L.5.2.
[12]Hiscock, *A Christ Church Miscellany,* 134-135.

records show that Oxford goldsmiths frequently acted as retailers for the work of London goldsmiths, but it is not so evident whether or not this was true a century and more earlier. It is obvious, however, that not all purchases were made from local goldsmiths as in 1610 payment was made for carriage of plate to be exchanged.[13]

In 1591 Magdalen paid Wright 55s. for eight spoons, and two years later he was paid £3/12/10 for silver vessels, and 5s. for mending a silver cup and five spoons. He did mending in 1600, and was paid £7 for two *cealerilj*. That same year he mended and gilded a cruet for 11s. 3d. In 1604, 1609 and 1610 he did various bits of mending and altering.[14] In 1612 he changed Dr. Chaloner's cup for 11s. 10d. and was also paid 47s. 6d. for changing a silver cup for ecclesiastical use.[15] It is likely that this was a chalice refashioned into a Communion cup, albeit rather belatedly, or it could have been a simple domestic wine goblet reshaped. In 1615, besides the usual repairing of plate, he engraved Walter Longe's coat-of-arms with the total cost being £4/7/0.[16]

Magdalen did not rely on William Wright nor any other Oxford goldsmith at this time for major purchases as in 1601 three silver cups were purchased from Richard Gossen, a London goldsmith in Foster Lane, for £20 plus 5s. 7d. for carriage, and in 1604 Gossen was paid £20/5/0, but the records lack a description of the goods.[17]

William Wright was employed by Oriel College in 1598, and in 1604 he was paid 44s. 6d. for a silver cruet.[18] It is not possible to determine if he were employed by any of the other colleges due to lack of records, except for a payment made by University College of 18s. 6d. at a date unrecorded. Since there is a payment of 10s. made to Thomas Crompton immediately following this entry, it would have to have been prior to 1625 when Crompton left Oxford.[19] It is likely that his other occupation as a baker took precedence.

Like so many of the Oxford goldsmiths, Wright became involved in local politics. He began this career in 1585 as constable, followed by

[13]Christ Church College MS. xii.b.54.

[14]Magdalen College MSS. LC7 and LCE8.

[15]W. D. Macray, *A Register of the Members of St. Mary Magdalen College, Oxford* (1897–1906), III, 42.

[16]Magdalen College MS. LCE8.

[17]Ibid., LC7.

[18]Oriel College's Treasurer's Accounts ETC B2.

[19]University College MSS.

election to the Common Council in 1596, and then as chamberlain two years later. From 1600 to 1607 he was repeatedly elected bailiff. In 1609 he was keeper of the five keys and two years later on the Mayor's Council, an office he held until 1625. January 19, 1618, he was chosen alderman in place of one who was deceased. For this he paid £10 to the City and 20s. to the Mayor's chief serjeant.[20] William Wright was mayor in 1614.[21] By 1617 he was referred to as gentleman when he was one of His Majesty's Justices of the Peace for Oxford.[22]

He, however, had found himself on the other side of the law when he ran afoul of the University Proctors who policed the City at night—another contention between Town and Gown. Proceedings were begun against him in the Chancellor's Court 5 November 1596 for breech of the peace, more specifically noctivagation (wandering the streets after curfew) and resistance to arrest. The matter was settled 18 November when Wright confessed and was excused the fine, but he had to pay 10s. 5d. costs.[23]

The chamberlain's accounts for 1604–1605 note that William Wright, goldsmith, was paid £14/13/0 for the cup given to the young prince and 16s. for exchanging £50 of money into gold which was to be put into the King's cup, the Queen's purse, and the Prince's cup[24] at the time of a royal visit. The accounts for 1627–1628 record payment by him of 35s. which the City had given him as reimbursement for a piece of plate which was lost at an entertainment for the Earl of Banbury and Lord Carleton. The object was later recovered and returned to Wright.[25]

An unmarked mace which is still part of the City Plate and is exhibited in the Museum of Oxford, is probably the work of William Wright. September 18, 1605 it was agreed that Baldwin Hodges would be sworn as sergeant to the Mayor and a crier of the City. The appointment was not without cost to Mr. Hodges, who had been made free of the City gratis September 13, 1593, as it was decreed that "he shall new make his mace at his owne charge and leave the same to the use of this Cytie at the time

[20]OCA, 1583–1626, 20 et passim.
[21]Wood, City of Oxford, 35, and Vide J. E. T. Rogers, Oxford City Documents, 1268–1665 (1891).
[22]OCA, 1583–1626, 267.
[23]University Archives 127v, 134r, 1596/58.
[24]OCA, 1583–1626, 389.
[25]OCA, 1626–1665, 412.

of his death or other departure from his offices."[26] Wright was a bailiff at this time, and by August 28, 1611, he held a tenement in St. Martin's parish next to one occupied by Baldwin Hodges.[27]

Wright served St. Martin's parish as churchwarden in 1594 and 1595, and as a vestryman for most years between 1596 and 1617. In 1619 he subscribed 10s. toward the clock and chimes, and in the church tax list of that year he paid 20s., both sums being larger than those paid by others.[28]

William Wright was obviously prospering as in 1602 the City granted him a lease for 41 years of garden in the town ditch toward Balliol College for which the fine was 40s.[29] March 18, 1606/7 the City rented him a garden and orchard in the Northeast Ward for £1, and a tenement near Brokenhays in the suburbs for 5s.[30] On October 13, 1606 Oriel College had granted a lease to William Wright, goldsmith, of 143 High Street and the family continued to hold the lease until 1760. The property had been rebuilt between 1579 and 1591.[31] As of June 18, 1613, he was to have a lease for 21 years of the garden which was then in the tenure of Michael Young, with a rent of 2s. 6d. The lease provided that a key of the door must be left at the City office for the use of the Mayor, Town Clerk and the rest of the Thirteen.[32] In 1625 he held a small stone house in Pennyfarthing Street which is now No. 12 Pembroke Street.[33] For a rent of 10s. and two capons he acquired a 40-year lease of two messuages, the eastern tenement, in St. Mary Magdalen parish August 10, 1630.[34]

A multitude of Wrights appear in the register of St. Martin's parish but the earliest entries are few. With some degree of certainty it can be ascertained that William Wright, goldsmith and baker, was the father of at least three children: Martin who became a goldsmith and added to the family fortune, baptized November 24, 1594; William, baptized April 12, 1606, and Margaret who was buried February 15, 1613/14. There is no

[26]OCA, 1583–1626, 80–81, 176.

[27]Salter, Oxford City Properties, 141.

[28]Oxon. Archives, D. D. Par. Oxford, St. Martin's a.1. (1540–1680).

[29]OCA, 1583–1626, 149.

[30]Salter, Oxford City Properties, 2, 7.

[31]Shadwell and Salter, Oriel College Records (1926), 256, and Salter, Survey of Oxford, I, 163.

[32]OCA, 1583–1626, 226.

[33]Salter, Survey of Oxford, II, 88.

[34]Salter, Oxford City Properties, 290.

Mace of the Mayor's Sergeant, 1606. Reproduced with permission of the Oxfordshire County Council, Museum of Oxford.

Detail of mace made in 1606 for Baldwin Hodges bearing his initials.

baptismal record for her. Mr. William Wright, alderman, as it is given in St. Martin's register, was buried February 28, 1635/6. According to Wood, he died February 26, and his wife, Joane Winter Wright had preceded him in death about 1616.[35]

---

[35]Wood, *City of Oxford*, 166.

Martin Wright

There is no apprenticeship record of Martin Wright, nor does his baptismal record at St. Martin's parish November 24, 1594, indicate that he was the son of William Wright, goldsmith. There is ample evidence, however, in other sources to prove this relationship. July 12, 1616, it was recorded in the Oxford Council Acts that Martin Wright, son and apprentice of William Wright, goldsmith, was admitted free and paid 4s. 6d.[1]

Beginning in that year the name of Martin Wright appears in the records of Christ Church College, displacing that of his father. In 1622, he was paid £2/12/8 for unspecified work.[2] Six years later he signed the Treasurer's Disbursement Book acknowledging receipt of £8/8/9 for a pot weighing "29 ounces a quarter six pence" at 5s. 9d. per ounce which was made from plate money.[3] The following year, in 1629, he was paid 41s. 3d. for mending done, and £13/10/8 for two pots with ears weighing 12d. less than 56 ounces. The cost of engraving was included in the price.[4] Wright's largest order from the college came the next year when he provided a basin and ewer weighing more than 111 ounces charged at 5s. 11d. per ounce and totalling £32/1/10. Against this cost an old basin and ewer were turned in which weighed just under 64 ounces for which he allowed 5s. per ounce yielding £15/15/7. Cost of engraving was 6s. 8d., so Martin Wright signed for receiving £16/12/11. That year he was also paid £4/16/7 for mending and changing plate, and 2s. 7d. for weighing the college plate at the audit.[5]

[1]OCA, 1583–1626, 258.
[2]Christ Church College MS. ii.b.67.
[3]Ibid., xii.b.73.
[4]Ibid., xii.b.74.
[5]Ibid., xii.75.

It is unfortunate that Magdalen, in the college accounts, did not distinguish among the members of the Wright family of goldsmiths who did work for the college from at least 1591 to 1662 when Daniel Porter became the college goldsmith. Since Martin's father William died in 1635, it is certain that entries in the bursar books later than that citing only "Mr. Wright" would have been Martin. Most of his work consisted of mending and cleaning, except for a silver rod in 1643 for which he was paid £1/6/0.[6]

The same situation prevailed at Corpus Christi College where payments for mending and changing plate were made to "Mr. Wright" between 1619 and 1644. In 1638, however, Martin Wright was paid £5/3/3 for a new salt and for mending and changing plate. It is interesting to note in that same year Parsons the Mercer was paid a shilling for sand and whiting to scour the plate.[7] At Oriel Martin Wright was employed between 1637 and 1642 repairing silver cups — three one year and four another year with the number unspecified in the other years.[8] One wonders why only the cups became battered. Between 1619 and 1633, "Mr. Wright" mended plate at Balliol.[9]

The accounts of the University Vice Chancellor vary considerably in specific details, and as with so many college accounts, only surnames are recorded. Only one payment by the University can be positively identified as being made to Martin Wright. That was in 1636–1637 when he supplied three boxes to contain the seal of the University to confer the Master of Arts degree on three foreign dignitaries. The cost was £2/11/0.[10]

Like his father, Martin Wright soon became involved in local government. He was given a bailiff's place September 18, 1626.[11] He continued as such and later as keykeeper until January 10, 1634/5 when he was chosen one of the assistants for which he was assessed £5. In September he was named to the Mayor's Council and the following year he was elected Mayor. Following his term he was again on the Mayor's Council and keykeeper.[12] Then in 1640, he was elected alderman, and was "sworne uppon the Chequer in the upper Hall and tooke three oaths, i.e., the

6Magdalen College MS. LCD3.
7Corpus Christi College Libri Magni.
8Oriel College Treasurer's Accounts.
9Balliol College Liber Bursarii, 1615–1662.
10University Archives, WPB/21/4.
11OCA, 1583–1626, 342.
12OCA, 1626–1665, 52.

Oathe of Aldermanshippe, the oathe of Supremacie, and the oath of Allegiance."[13] He continued in these various City offices, again being elected Mayor in 1655, and the following year his son William succeeded him as Mayor, but he still was holding office as an alderman until the year of his death.[14]

Martin Wright's political career was not without its hazards. In 1644, while serving on the Mayor's Council, he and two others were imprisoned by the House of Lords. The Mayor and others presented a petition to the Lords and an interview with Lord Fleetwood accomplished their purpose. The three were reimbursed as they had suffered for the City.[15] In spite of this generous attitude on the part of the City, transgressions of the rules did not go unnoticed nor unpunished. August 14, 1652, Alderman Martin Wright as well as six other members of the House were each fined 4d. for coming to the Council in their cloaks.[16] It must have been a cold August.

With the coming of the Restoration, Martin Wright and son William, both aldermen, took the oath of allegiance to His Majesty Charles II on May 24, 1660, and the following day Martin Wright was one of those chosen to carry the "Gratulacon and Peticon" to the King in London with their expenses being paid by the City.[17] Like the Vicar of Bray, he seemed to go with which either way the wind blew. In other words, he always managed to be on the winning side, and this trait was also pronounced in his son William.

The Wrights threw themselves into preparations in 1661 for the King's anticipated visit to the City during his progress through the Kingdom, or perhaps they had no real choice in the matter; however, thinking in the County had changed by 1660. They and three other aldermen were to appear in scarlet gowns and tippets replete with footmen and footclothes.[18] Martin Wright had contributed £10 toward the £520 presented to Charles I by the City when he came to Oxford from Edgehill Battle[19] and ensconced himself at Christ Church. it must be admitted, however, that in view of the subsequent career of Martin's son William it cannot be

[13]*Ibid.*, 92.
[14]*Ibid.*, 103 et passim.
[15]*Ibid.*, xxviii, 126–127.
[16]*Ibid.*, 190.
[17]*Ibid.*, 261.
[18]*Ibid.*, 284.
[19]*Ibid.*, 379.

determined with certainty exactly where the Wrights stood during the course of the Civil War. Although no documents have been found to throw light on the matter, it is possible that the whitebaking trade of his father was carried on by Martin Wright. Supplying bread to the troops of either or both sides would have been very lucrative.

The City took advantage of Martin Wright's trade of goldsmith. September 27, 1625, it was recorded in the Council Acts that he had provided "two faier pieces of plate" which the City intended to present to the King and Queen when they came to Oxford. The plague, though, caused the plan to fall apart. The King, staying at Christ Church, feared infection and so refused to see the Mayor bearing the City's gifts. Martin Wright, therefore, was left holding the bag, so to speak. The City apparently had no intention of paying for the plate until after the presentation, so Wright was left with the intended gifts which he had purchased in London. The City, recognizing the style and workmanship of the plate may go out of fashion before another need arose for the objects, paid Wright £5 to keep them for several months. If during that time an occasion for their use presented itself then Wright would have to forfeit a proportionate amount of the £5.[20] The need apparently did not arise.

In 1629 it was thought that the King and Queen would be coming to Oxford, so the City Fathers decided that a gilt cup of the value of £30 to £40 would be presented to the King in spite of the fact that the City did not have the money for this and other gifts. It, therefore, became necessary to borrow the money. The Mayor lent £70. After other bills were paid the £15 left was given to Martin Wright in part payment for the plate given to the King. In 1630 he was paid £31/1/6 for the cup.[21]

The city was perpetually in dire financial straits, and when the High Steward of the City, Lord Howard, Earl of Berkshire, was desirous of borrowing £200 from the City in 1643–1644 the purse was empty. Anxious to please Lord Howard, the Mayor and three others, including Alderman Martin Wright who were members of the Mayor's Council, disposed of the City plate without the consent of the whole Council. The plate lost consisted of two tankards, one great pully salt, two trencher salts, two beer bowls, two Spanish cups and 12 spoons having a total value of £40/1/10.[22] The difference apparently was made up by those involved.

[20]*OCA, 1583–1626*, 333–334, 427, lxii.
[21]*OCA, 1626–1665*, 20–23, 414.
[22]*Ibid.*, xxii.

The Mayor died and the survivors were sued for the recovery of the plate with the legal expenses to be paid by the City. The matter dragged on and in 1652 a writ of arrest was issued, but apparently not enforced.

By September 1655, when Martin Wright was elected Mayor, it was found that the plate was worth £80. The matter was finally settled by deciding that £80 should be paid to the City by the miscreants and distributed thus: £20 to the Earl of Berkshire for three years' fees as High Steward, £20 to Mr. Dennis, one of the culprits, for six months' salary as Mayor, with the remaining £40 to be spent on new plate. The City gave the three survivors of this debacle the privilege of suing the Earl of Berkshire in the name of the City, but at their own expense to recoup the sum they had been forced to pay the City.[23]

In the midst of these difficulties, Wright made another loan of £50 to the City on April 27, 1646.[24] In 1628, he had lent £4/10/0 to St. Martin's parish and was repaid 10s. A payment of 6s. 8d. on the parish indebtness to him was made in 1634, but there is no record of further reimbursement. He first was chosen for the vestry at St. Martin's in 1622, and served a number of years until 1645.[25]

Martin Wright had a few less spectacular dealings with the City. In 1630–1631 he was paid £1/17/6 for an unspecified piece of plate, and in 1634–1635 he earned £2/8/10 "for making two maces and for making a new mace."[26] This is strangely worded; it is possible that the first instance should read "for mending two maces." At any rate they would have been small ones such as those carried by lesser officials. On March 24, 1663 the City reimbursed him £10 for the payment he had made to the University for the necessary repairs of the waterworks. A year later he was dead and his son, Alderman William Wright, replaced him as coroner, and John White, brewer, was elected to fill his place as one of the Commissioners of the Barges.[27]

Coupled with all his other activities, two apprentices of Martin Wright are recorded. John Slater [or Slatter] of Tetsworth, Oxon. was apprenticed for a term of ten years October 31, 1631.[28] The other one, of whom no apprenticeship record has been found, was Edward Cluett who served

[23]*Ibid.*, 152, 166, 192, 210.
[24]*Ibid.*, 458.
[25]Oxon. Archives, D.D. Par. Oxford. St. Martin's a.1 (1540–1680).
[26]*OCA, 1626–1665*, 414, 418.
[27]*Ibid.*, 306, 321.
[28]Hanaster Book, 1613–1640, L.5.2.

123

an apprenticeship of more than seven years and who was admitted free February 7, 1632/3.[29]

The lease granted to his father by Oriel in 1606 of 143 High Street passed to Martin.[30] An orchard to the south of Thomas Berry's property at 118–119 High Street in All Saints parish was held by Martin Wright in 1652,[31] and he held a tenement in High Street in St. Martin's parish which had been in the tenure of his father from at least 1611.[32] His father's lease in St. Mary Magdalen parish also passed to him, and on January 15, 1662/3 he assigned the residue of this lease to John Hopkins and John Crosse for £156/10/0.[33] A New College tenement called the Talbot at 28–29 Queen Street had been leased to Martin Wright October 18, 1637. It was probably destroyed in the fire of 1644.[34]

Martin Wright died May 14, 1664 and was buried in the chancel of St. Martin's Church, his grave marked with a marble stone on which was engraved, "Here enterred resteth the body of that worthy citizen Martin Wright alderman and twice mayor of this citie of Oxford. He departed this life May 14 an. dom. 1664 being of the age of 70 yeares." His wife, buried there August 3, 1643, was Katherine Medhop of Medhop Hall in Yorkshire. Martin, having no arms of his own, was buried with those of his wife. Seven sons and daughters and other members of his family also were buried in the church.[35] No evidence of their graves remains today as all that is left standing of St. Martin's Church is Carfax Tower.

When Martin wrote his will April 18, 1664, describing himself as one of the Aldermen of the City of Oxford, only five of his ten children were surviving. Named first was his daughter, Mary (who died unmarried in 1671), who was bequeathed all his lands in the parish of St. Giles in the suburbs of the City of Oxford held of lease of St. John's College. She also was to receive the first three years' benefit or profit of any monies due or payable out of certain lands in Waterperry in the County of Oxford, and three bonds due. His daughter Katherine Seaman (who died in 1680) was to receive the fourth year's profit from the Waterperry lands, and after

[29]OCA, 1626–1665, 38.
[30]Shadwell and Salter, Oriel College Records, 256.
[31]Salter, Oxford City Properties, 127.
[32]Ibid., 141.
[33]Ibid., 290.
[34]Salter, Survey of Oxford, II, 138.
[35]Wood, Survey of the Antiquities of the City of Oxford, 166–168; Wood, Life and Times, II, 12.

that his twelve grandchildren would receive these proceeds calculated at £26/13/4 each with certain provisions. To his loving son-in-law, Richard Croke (husband of his daughter Elizabeth) he provided for "a peec of silver Plate of Twenty pounds price to be after the newest fashion being a Chase stand with a Chased pott with two yeares [ears] in the middle of the dish to bee delivered within one yeare after my decease."

Fourteen relatives were given gold rings valued at 20s. to wear for his sake. The sum of £40 was willed to the poor of Oxford. His plate, linen, bedding, all furniture, brass, pewter and household goods was to be divided among his five children, William, Katherine Seaman, Elizabeth Croke, Mary Wright, and Grace Nurse, with Mary receiving the largest portion. To the City of Oxford he left the sum of £10 toward the making of the stairs up to the Council Chamber, to be paid when the work began. His beloved son William was appointed sole executor with no overseers. The will was probated in the Prerogative Court of Canterbury June 24, 1664.[36]

[36]P.R.O., P.C.C. Will [77 Bruce] Prob. 11/314.

William Wright II

The third member of the Wright goldsmithing dynasty was William Wright II or sometimes referred to as William Wright the Elder. The son of Martin and Katherine Wright, he was baptized at St. Martin's June 29, 1619. There is no record of his apprenticeship nor of his freedom, but it may be assumed that he was apprenticed to his father circa 1634.

From extant records, it appears that he did little work as a goldsmith. When only the surname appears, it is not totally possible to differentiate between William II and his father, Martin, or between William and his cousin, Alexander. Such is the case with the payment of 6s. 9d. "To Mr. Wright Goldsmith his bill" recorded by University College April 18, 1688.[1] At Oriel, however, he is well documented as following his father's employment there. In 1653 he was paid 6s. 4d., presumably for mending. Two years later his bill was 16s. 6d. for mending a small silver vessel, and in 1658 he was paid 18s. 6d. In 1660 he did his last work for the college for which he collected £5/1/0, but unfortunately the work is not described. After that year his former apprentice, Daniel Porter, became Oriel's goldsmith.[2] Wright had only one other apprentice, William Chillingworth, son of Ralph Chillingworth, of the City of Oxford, brewer, who was apprenticed October 17, 1657.[3] There is no further reference to him. In 1654 Mr. Wright was paid 10s. for repairing a silver cup at Magdalen, but again it is not clear which Mr. Wright this was.[4]

William Wright apparently was not employed by any of the other colleges. Two entries in the Vice-Chancellor's accounts may or may not apply to him. In the accounts for the academic year beginning September 8, 1650, the University paid "Mr. Wright Goldsmith" 17s. 6d. for a box for

[1]University College MSS.
[2]Oriel College Treasurer's Accounts.
[3]Hanaster Book, 1639–1662, L.5.3.
[4]Macray, *A Register of the Members of St. Mary Magdalen College, Oxford*, IV, 9.

the seal of the patent sent to the Chancellor. Three years later the bill of Mr. Wright Goldsmith" was £4/8/0 for mending and new gilding the staff belonging to the Superior Bedel in Divinity.[5]

The City utilized his services in 1646–1647 when he received payment of £10/2/4 for two silver tankards presented to the Governor, and in 1651–1652, he and Thomas Berry benefitted when the keykeepers made payment of £2/6/0 toward the cost of the new mace. This probably referred to merely removing the Royal Arms and replacing them with the Arms of the Commonwealth. In 1664–1665, 13s. 6d. was the cost of mending a tankard, 12 spoons, and a new staff for the constable of the Northeast Ward.[6]

Wright did not seem much interested in his goldsmithing trade. Politics had more appeal for him; and, his particular brand of politics may have been a contributing factor to his lack of patronage by the Royalist University Establishment. He entered politics with his father, but was destined to play a more vociferous and controversial rôle than had Martin Wright. In 1650 he was bailiff,[7] and by 1656 he was one of the eight assistants when he succeeded his father as Mayor. May 24, 1660 Martin and William Wright, along with others, took the oath of allegiance to Charles II, and in that same year they were both on the Mayor's Council as well as in 1662. In 1664 he took his late father's place as coroner,[8] and was forced to surrender the office in 1667,[9] but he was again Mayor in that year.[10] The City borrowed £150 from his wife in 1663–1664, and the next year paid her £9 interest on the money.[11]

In the course of his political career he was described as fond of cock-fighting, as indeed were all the City Fathers; as a firebrand, and according to Wood, clownish and ill-natured. When James, Duke of Monmouth, was given the freedom of the City September 18, 1680, the University ignored him, but Wright and some of his cohorts called out, "God save him and the Protestant religion." The following February he was elected to the Third Parliament, having served in the two short-lived previous Whig Parliaments. This one, which met in Oxford, also had a short life.

[5]University Archives, WPB/21/4.
[6]OCA, 1626–1665, 431–449.
[7]Wood, Survey, 38.
[8]OCA, 1626–1665, 321.
[9]OCA, 1666–1701, 70.
[10]Ibid., 14.
[11]OCA, 1626–1665, 447, 451.

In 1661, the ancient quarrel between Town and Gown was resurrected when the University presented a list of grievances to the King who ruled against the City. Twenty years later William Wright instigated a new revolt over one of the old issues; i.e., the observance of St. Scholastica's Day, and demanded a petition be sent to Parliament. There was not a full attendance at St. Mary's. The Mayor and twenty others did attend, but others refused in order to show their contempt. The next year there was a full attendance of the citizenry as Wright had told them a hole might be picked in their charter if they did not appear.

In 1683 the Charter was surrendered. All officers of the City now held their office at the pleasure of the King and they were forced to take the oath of allegiance and supremacy. The whole corporation was turned out by James II in 1687. William Wright had resigned his position as alderman and his freedom a few months after the charter was surrendered. Earlier in the year he had been imprisoned by Judge Jeffreys.[12] He had been suspected in the Rye house plot. As a consequence, at eight o'clock in the evening of June 25, 1683, Lord Norrys, eldest son of the Earl of Abingdon, along with others including constables searched his home as well as that of Lawrence King, the anabaptist father of Lemuel King, goldsmith, looking for arms. The search continued in the morning, and Wright's house was searched again on July 17, but no arms were found.[13] The ardent anti-Royalist and Whig apparently played his cards right as in 1688, at the King's pleasure, he was readmitted to his freedom and was to be one of the two new aldermen although his name does not appear in the September list of that year.[14]

The leases which were held at the time of Martin Wright's death passed on to his eldest son, William. In addition, on April 20, 1664 he was given a lease of the City of a moiety in the parish of St. Thomas, Cripley, for 21 years with rent 45s. and two capons. The lease was renewed in 1672, 1678, and for a fine of £17/10/0 in 1685. On March 1, 1693 it was renewed by his son William for a like fine. This son, the Recorder of Oxford, on August 29, 1701, was granted a lease for the whole of Cripley for forty years, rent £4/10/0, and fine £45 after 8½ years. This lease did not pass from the family until 1799.[15] In 1668 William Wright, goldsmith

[12]*OCA, 1666–1701*, introduction.
[13]Wood, *Life*, III, 59, 62.
[14]*OCA, 1666–1701*, introduction.
[15]Salter, *Oxford City Properties*, 192–193.

and alderman, obtained a lease of two messuages in St. Michael's parish on the west side of Northgate for forty years, rent 40s. and two capons.[16]

Rentals of City properties included a house and garden on the north side of Exeter College in 1658, 2s. 6d., and in the same year, a cellar and window in St. Martin's parish, 5s., as well as a garden and house of office in Guild Hall Court, 13s. 4d.[17] The property near Exeter College was a large house built in 1636 by Dr. Prideaux, with a frontage of 71 feet according to the Survey of 1772. In the Hearth Tax of 1665, it had the unusually large number of thirteen hearths, and it had 20 windows. The lease was granted in 1668, and renewed in 1682 with the addition of a building which was erected on a tower of the wall called Dr. Holland's Tower. It adjoined the west part of the tenement of the north side of the college chapel.[18] This remained the home of the Wright family for succeeding generations until the freehold was sold to Exeter College in 1773.[19] In 1667 the City granted a new lease to Wright of The Three Goats Heads.[20] February 16, 1669, he paid a languable of 6d. for two posts before his house in All Saints parish at 124 and 123 High Street which was called The Bear. He must have been the owner.[21] William Wright had expanded the estate left by his father. In the Poll Tax of 1667 he paid a guinea, plus £4 on money, and 9s. for his wife and eight children.[22]

The life of William Wright II came to an end in 1693. He was buried November 2 in the chancel of St. Martin's which he had served as churchwarden in 1649, and vestryman four years between 1650 and 1657.[23] His first wife was Christian Smith, daughter of John Smith, gentleman, of St. Aldate's where they were married in 1646. She was buried at St. Martin's June 26, 1656. Their daughter, also named Christian, was buried February 20, 1650/1, having been baptized December 5, 1649. His second wife was Mary Banks, widow of _____ Dew of Islip.[24] She died June 13, 1696, age 76, and was buried June 17 at St. Peter-in-the-East.

---

[16]*Ibid.*, 236.
[17]*Ibid.*, 9–11.
[18]*Ibid.*, 281; OCA, *1666–1701,* 137, 359.
[19]Salter, *Oxford City Properties,* 281.
[20]OCA, *1666–1701,* 28.
[21]Salter, *Survey of Oxford,* I, 175.
[22]Salter, *Surveys and Tokens,* 232.
[23]Oxon. Archives, D.D. Par. Oxford. St. Martin's A.1. (1540–1680).
[24]Wood, *Survey,* 166–167.

William Wright, styling himself William Wright the Elder, had written his will July 28, 1690. In it he named his son Martin as heir to his lease of Oriel College, the garden near the Hall held of the City of Oxford, and the lease and estate held of the Right Honourable the Earl of Abingdon for his land and herediments in Chesterton and Windlebury in the County of Oxford with the profits of the rents for the first two years to be paid to his wife to be used toward the payment of his debts. Martin also was bequeathed the lease and estate held of Corpus Christi College for certain lands and tenements in Hanborough, Oxon. His son, William, Recorder of Oxford, received his moiety of Cripley held by lease of the City of Oxford, and his half-part of a lease held of the Dean and Chapter of Christ Church for the tithes of Cripley and Sidelands. Wright also held a lease of Magdalen College of lands at Garsington, certain lands and tenements in Oxford held of a lease of Mr. Furse of Devonshire, and two houses against Lincoln College held of a lease of Christ Church College. His wife, Mary, was to receive these as well as the "house I now live in held of the City of Oxon." Further bequests were made to other of his relatives and children including his daughter Alice Harris, the only other child by his first wife, who was baptized at St. Martin's July 22, 1647, and his cousin, Alexander Wright. Mrs. Mary Wright, "my truly loving wife," was appointed sole executrix and his son William and his son-in-law John Dewe as overseers.

Shortly before his death he had second thoughts about his lands at Hanborough. Instead of Martin as heir, they were left in trust to his wife with certain provisions. The codicil was written October 25, 1693, and by then William Wright was too ill to sign it, making only his mark. The will was probated November 22, 1693 in the Prerogative Court of Canterbury.[25]

[25]P.R.O., P.C.C. Will [199 Coker] Prob. 11/417. It is possible that Wood erred in stating that Wright's second wife was the widow of _____ Dew, as a son-in-law's surname was Dewe; however, he could have been a step-son-in-law. Wood also stated that Wright was 98 at the time of his death when he was actually only 74.

Alexander Wright I

Alexander Wright was a son of William Wright, gentleman, who was a son of William Wright I, goldsmith, a nephew of Martin Wright, goldsmith, and a cousin of William Wright II, goldsmith. He was baptized at All Saints April 17, 1634. As was customary, his mother's name is not given. It may have been Dorothy who was buried May 26, 1686 at St. Martin's where she is listed in the parish register as wife of William Wright, Esq.

Alexander was apprenticed to Samuel Wilkins of the City of Oxford, goldsmith, for a term of eight years November 1, 1649. He gained his freedom September 20, 1658.[1] There is no indication that he did any work for the colleges or the University. He was, however, active with work for the City.

In 1667–1668 he was paid 19s. 2d. for mending the City plate, as well as being paid 10s. for the loss of a piece of plate which he had made for the City's use. The following year the cost was 11s. for work done on the mace and for silver spoons. The bill was 16s. 2d. for mending the City plate the next year. In 1670–1671 he was paid 18s. 6d. for engraving "ye Oxe Seale in silver" by the order of the Mayor. The following year he mended and regilt the top of the Great Mace at a cost of £18/2/8. He was paid in 1675–1676 £14/3/9 for new badges for the City waits and Alderman Harris's pensioners and for other unspecified things. (Alderman Harris was a son-in-law of Alderman William Wright II). Two years later he provided a new mace for Alexander Cosier, victualler, serjeant-at-mace to the junior bailiff, and changed three tankards for which he charged £5/14/8.[2] His greatest involvement with his craft was in the making of a new mace for the City after the Restoration. This has been discussed in the chapter, *John Slatter*.

[1] Hanaster Book, 1639–1662, L.5.3.
[2] *OCA, 1666–1701, 57, 320–333.*

In 1688 he was summoned to appear at Goldsmiths' Hall for selling one gold ring worse than standard, but did not appear in person. Lawrence Coles, London goldsmith, stood in for him informing the court he had orders from Wright that the consideration of his case be left up to the Court. As a result he was ordered to pay 13s. 8d., the cost of the ring, and 5s. as a fine. The ring was returned to him defaced.[3] As a major trade supplier of spoons, Coles must have been selling to Wright.

Like his relatives, Alexander Wright was soon involved in the governance of the City. From 1661 to 1667 he served on the Common Council, in the latter year becoming senior chamberlain and continuing as such until becoming senior bailiff in 1674. He continued in this post until 1693. In 1689 he was fined 20s. for not appearing at Council; nevertheless, in 1693 he was chosen as one of the eight assistants to fill the place of one deceased. By the next year, however, he apparently was either tired of or disenchanted with holding office as on November 29, 1694, it was noted in the Council Acts that "the Mayor and his brethren are to treat with Mr. Alex. Wright in order to bring him to attend his place as assistant or resign." He hung on to his office until 1696 when on December 3 it was decided that the High Steward should be acquainted with the fact, as soon as possible, that Alexander Wright was neglecting his office, and added that "his lordship is requested to use such methods as he thinks suitable to compel Mr. Wright to do his duty." He resigned his office January 31 and a week later paid his fine after further threats. April 21, 1699, Alexander Wright resigned his freedom and paid 20s.[4] His career was over.

Alexander's wife, Katherine, was buried at St. Martin's September 19, 1680. They were the parents of five children, only one of whom survived their father. All were baptized at St. Martin's: Mary, March 31, 1668, buried September 27, 1674; Elizabeth, born September 30, 1673 and baptized October 12, 1673, buried November 24, 1674; Alexander, baptized March 14, 1661/2, buried March 5, 1678/9; Martin, baptized April 17, 1666, buried June 6, 1689, and William, baptized July 3, 1670.

Alexander Wright married again. His second wife was Sarah Ewstace Eagleton, a wealthy widow who held lands in Wooton Underwood, Buckinghamshire, on which there were houses, gardens, orchards, barns, sta-

---

[3]Goldsmiths' Company, Court Minute Book 10, p. 4a. July 6, 1688. His name is given as Abraham, but the reference must have been to Alexander.
[4]OCA, 1626–1665, 288–328.

bles and other buildings. She also had approximately four acres at Ham in the County of Bucks. The marriage took place November 5, 1683 at St. Aldate's with a prenuptial agreement being confirmed. She died in 1689 leaving a long, complicated will by which Alexander was bequeathed £200 to be distributed to him at the rate of £50 per year for four years. The will was probated in the Prerogative Court of Canterbury October 23, 1689.[5]

Alexander was not as financially well-off as his more prominent relatives. In the Hearth Tax of 1665 he was listed in St. Martin's parish in the Southeast Ward as having six hearths.[6] He was assessed 2s. for himself and his wife in the Poll Tax of 1667, and 2s. for their children, Alexander and Martin.[7] His name does not appear in any of the leases of the City.

His eldest son, Alexander, was apprenticed to him November 1, 1676 for a term of seven years, but he died less than three years later at the age of 17. There is no apprenticeship record for William, but he was admitted to the freedom of the City in 1695 when he was described as "filius natur maximus Alexander Wright, goldsmith."[8] This William carried on the goldsmithing tradition of the family well into the eighteenth century.

Alexander Wright had two apprentices who were not members of the family. Lawrence Taylor, son of John Taylor of the City of Oxford, tobacco pipemaker, began a seven-year term July 5, 1666 and was admitted free July 7, 1677. Nothing more is known of him. Richard Dubber, son of Richard Dubber late of Wolvercote in the County of Oxford, yeoman, was apprenticed June 25, 1667 for a term of seven years.[9]

Alexander Wright was 67 years old when he died, and was buried at St. Martin's September 12, 1701, leaving no will. Having buried two wives and four children it is not surprising that he neglected his civic duties toward the end of his life.

[5]P.R.O., P.C.C. Will [137 Ent] Prob. 11/396.
[6]Salter, *Surveys and Tokens*, 186.
[7]*Ibid.*, 222.
[8]Hanaster Book, 1662–1699, L.5.4.
[9]*Ibid.*

William Wright III

William Wright III, baptized July 3, 1670, at St. Martin's was the son of Alexander Wright, goldsmith, and his wife, Katherine. There is no record of apprenticeship, but he was admitted free in 1695.[1]

His earliest recorded work was for Oriel College in 1712. From then until 1724 the payments for unspecified work varied from a few shillings to slightly over a pound, but in the last year he was paid £3/4/0.[2] Scarcely more than a pound were the payments made by Exeter in 1714–1715 and in 1715–1716, but in 1717–1718, the college paid Wright £53/12/9 for changing and mending plate, plus 3s. 6d. on another bill.[3] His employment at Pembroke was extremely brief; i.e., one payment of 11s. in 1722–1723.[4]

Already Wright had been summoned to Goldsmiths' Hall to answer charges for selling substandard goods. June 26, 1706 Mr. Lee appeared for him before the court to answer the charge of selling substandard unspecified gold wares. The result was that he was forced to pay £1/3/6, the cost of the goods, but the £3 charges were excused.[5] The next time the Court was not so lenient and he appeared in person. The charge was for selling substandard gold and silver wares. September 17, 1719 he paid £7/15/6 which represented a fine and the cost of the goods, which were defaced.[6] He apparently learned his lesson as there are no further appearances before the Court. It appears from these entries that he had a retail shop, but it is uncertain whether he actually made the goods he sold.

[1]Hanaster Book, 1662–1699, L.5.4.
[2]Oriel College Treasurers' Accounts.
[3]Exeter College A.II.10 (1639–1734).
[4]Pembroke College 4.3.3.
[5]Goldsmiths' Company Court Minute Book 10, p. 309a. Samuel Lee, London goldsmith, whose first mark was entered as a largeworker in 1701.
[6]*Ibid.*, Court Minute Book 12, p. 10.

William Wright III did not share the enthusiasm for municipal service exhibited by earlier members of his family. September 30, 1701 William Wright, goldsmith, and Martin Wright, gentleman, were elected bailiffs, and were elected to fill up the 24. On taking their oaths they each paid 3s. 4d. for not being constables, and it was agreed they should have bailiffs' places, each paying £15. Both held this office until 1709 when William Wright was elected senior bailiff, but he asked to be excused and to be dismissed from further attendance. Following discussion of the matter, his request was granted and a fine of £30 was levied.[7] Neither he nor Martin served any further.

This Martin Wright was a son of William Wright II, Mayor and goldsmith, and brother of William Wright, Recorder. He died in 1711 unmarried, leaving his brother as executor of his estate.[8]

All that is known about William Wright's property comes from the Sun Fire Insurance records. July 15, 1718 he insured his malt house in the parish of St. Aldate's which was in the possession of Christopher Easton. The premium was 7s. each on the goods and merchandise in the dwelling house.[9] August 22, 1729 he took out a policy on his house, back kitchen and room over it, stone and slated in the parish of St. Aldate's which was in the tenure of John Suggins, cook at Christ Church College, value not exceeding £140. He also insured his house only "in the Same Side," stone and slated, in the tenure of John Griffin, tailor, not exceeding £80. Also insured was one other house only in the same backside, stone and timber and slated, in the tenure of Francis Knight, goldsmith, not exceeding £40. Two stables and a woodhouse in the same backside belonging to the aforesaid houses which were timber and slated, not exceeding £40. The total valuation was £300.[10] September 8, 1730 he insured a dwelling house in Little Milton in the parish of Great Milton for £100 with £40 on the household goods therein. The barn and coach house were insured for £40, hay and corn thrashed £50, the pidgeon loft £20, two stables £40, and three cowhouses £10 for a total of £300.[11] On all these policies Wright is listed as of the parish of St. Martin's, Oxford.

[7]*OCA, 1701–1752*, 2–53.
[8]Oxon. Archives, W.206.69; 73/4/30.
[9]London Guildhall MS. 11936, vol. 8, 155.
[10]*Ibid.*, vol. 29, n.p.
[11]*Ibid.*, vol. 30, 479.

William Wright III and Lydia Carter were married July 22, 1694 at St. Aldate's. A son, Alexander, was born April 15, 1695 and baptized at St. Martin's on May 5. Lydia, their daughter, was born March 2, 1695/6, and baptized March 22, but lived only a short time, being buried at St. Martin's May 26, 1696. Another daughter, Catherine, was baptized at St. Martin's July 14, 1706.

The last mention of this William Wright was in the late autumn of 1730 when he successfully sued a group of men for £59/12/2 debt and damage in the Chancellor's Court. The suit was begun 16 October and settled 13 November.[12]

There was yet another Alexander Wright, goldsmith, whose widow, Elizabeth, wrote her will in 1725 and it was probated February 8, 1732/3. A deed of settlement had been executed before their marriage. She was the daughter of John Hughes, deceased, of Burford, beside whom she was to be buried. Her only survivors were her sister and a nephew. To her sister Rebekah Jackson of Oxford she bequeathed all her jewels, plate, linen, household goods, debts, and all other of her estate.[13] It is possible that this Alexander was the son of William Wright III who was born in 1695. This, however, would have made him only thirty years old when Elizabeth, already widowed, wrote her will.

[12]University Archives 1730/118, 196r, 204v.
[13]Oxon. Archives, W.210.45; 157/4/34.

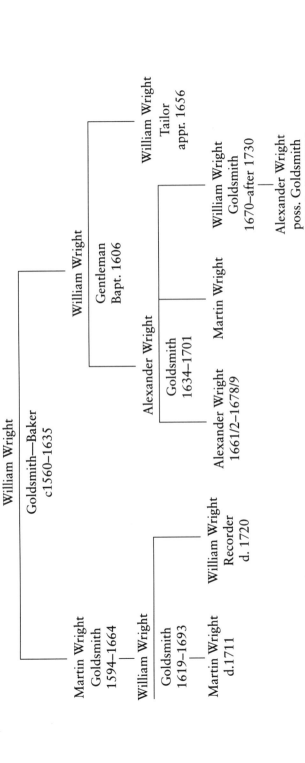

William Wright
Goldsmith—Baker
c1560–1635

Martin Wright
Goldsmith
1594–1664

William Wright

William Wright
Gentleman
Bapt. 1606

William Wright
Tailor
appr. 1656

William Wright
Goldsmith
1619–1693

William Wright
Recorder
d. 1720

Alexander Wright
Goldsmith
1634–1701

Martin Wright
d.1711

Alexander Wright
1661/2–1678/9

Martin Wright

William Wright
Goldsmith
1670–after 1730

Alexander Wright
poss. Goldsmith
1695–before 1725

John de Gruchy

John de Gruchy advertised in *Jackson's Oxford Journal* 18 June 1763 that he was a goldsmith from London who had opened shop near the Printing House. Son of the Reverend Philip de Gruchy of the Island of Jersey, deceased, he was apprenticed for a term of seven years to John Swift under the London Company 4 October 1758 on payment of £50.[1] He may have been a native of St. Helier, Jersey, as Thomas de Gruchy, goldsmith, was working there at 2 Brook Street, circa 1822. He also sold long-case clocks.[2]

De Gruchy's master, John Swift, made more silver for the Oxford colleges in the eighteenth century than any other London goldsmith.[3] It is highly probable that Swift told him how much work for a goldsmith there was in Oxford, but it is unknown why his apprenticeship ended two years short of term. It is possible that Swift died. The date of his death is not recorded and there is confusion arising from the fact that his son, John, was also a goldsmith. De Gruchy received his freedom in Oxford 28 March 1763, paying twelve guineas and official fees.[4]

Between 1763 and 1766 he did mending of plate at Brasenose, and that is the only reference to his work. He does, however, appear in the Parliamentary Report list of 1773 as a goldsmith in Oxford. By 1779, though, he was back in London where he registered his first mark as a small-worker in partnership with Alexander Field 20 April 1779 with the address, City Road. By 14 July 1780, the partnership was apparently dissolved when Field entered a separate mark.[5] De Gruchy did not enter a separate mark, so he may have died or returned to Jersey. He had given Oxford a fair trial of more than sixteen years but he probably found that

[1]Goldsmiths' Company Apprenticeship Book 7.
[2]Richard Mayne, *Channel Islands Silver*, 2nd ed. (1985), 47.
[3]E. A. Jones, *Catalogue of the Plate of Magdalen College, Oxford* (1940), xv.
[4]*OCA, 1752–1801*, 51.
[5]A. G. Grimwade, *London Goldsmiths, 1697–1837*, 2nd ed. (1982), 487.

the goldsmiths who came from Oxfordshire families and who had served their apprenticeships in Oxford were favoured by the colleges and perhaps by the townspeople as well.

De Gruchy had been in Oxford little more than three years when Mrs. de Gruchy placed the following advertisement in *Jackson's Oxford Journal* 5 September 1767:

> Young Ladies are carefully and expeditiously Taught French, by Mrs. de Gruchy, at Mr. Gruchy's, silversmith, opposite the King's Arms, the corner of Holiwell, Oxford, leading to the Parks.
>
> The Terms are Half a Guinea a Quarter and Half a Guinea Entrance.
>
> N.B. Young Gentlemen, educated in any of the Schools in Oxford, may likewise be taught at convenient opportunities.

She probably felt the need to add to the family income.

John Gavey

John Gavey, like John de Gruchy, could be termed a bird of passage, but there is much less known about him. Listed as a silversmith, he purchased his freedom for 20 guineas 25 June 1756.[1]

Gavey placed an advertisement in *Jackson's Oxford Journal* 31 December 1757 proclaiming his talents as a working silver- and goldsmith. He was situated near St. Mary's Church in the High Street, and went on to say that he "makes, mends, sells, and performs all Branches relating to that Business, in the best, most fashionable, and cheapest Manner," but he did not tell his readers anything about his former domicile.

Also like John de Gruchy, John Gavey was probably a native of Jersey and son of Jean Gavey, a prolific and excellent silversmith who flourished circa 1715 to 1775. His premises were in King Street, St. Helier, Jersey. Jean Gavey had a son, Edouard, also a silversmith, who first worked in Jersey and then by 1755, was established in Dolphin Court, Ludgate Hill, London.[2]

John Gavey may have had some business with the townspeople of Oxford, but there is little mention of work for the colleges. In 1759 Oriel found need for his services,[3] and Magdalen, the same year, paid him £2/14/6.[4] He was probably gone by 3 May 1760, when an advertisement appeared in the *Oxford Journal* for a "house to let, corner Holywell, late in possession of Gavey, silversmith." This may have been the house later occupied by de Gruchy.

It is possible that Gavey returned to Jersey as Mayne lists Jean Gavey as flourishing circa 1715 to 1775. This means that he was still flourishing in his eighties which is highly unlikely. It is more probable that the later

---

[1]*OCA, 1752–1801,* 17.
[2]Mayne, *Channel Islands Silver,* 55–57. He is not listed in Grimwade nor Heal.
[3]Oriel College Treasurer's Accounts, 1.E.17.
[4]Magdalen College Bursar's Book.

work bearing the crowned I·G mark was the work of his presumed son, John Gavey, late of Oxford. It is tantalizing to speculate if among the stock he had for sale was some of the work of Jean Gavey and Edouard Gavey.

There was an alliance between the Gavey and de Gruchy families as evidenced by an Oxford Diocesan marriage bond 28 April 1755. John Gavey of Swerford, silversmith, age 30, married Ann de Gruchy, age 24, also of Swerford. The place of the ceremony was not specified.[5] It is unfortunate that the names of the couple's parents are not recorded. The bride, approximately twelve years older than John de Gruchy, must have been his sister. If this were the relationship she was in Swerford at least three years before John was apprenticed in London, and the question arises—why was she living in this tiny village north of Chipping Norton? The same question could be asked about John Gavey. It was the very next year that he purchased his freedom in Oxford, so it is likely that he and his bride then took up residence in the City.

[5]Oxon. Archives, Oxf. dioc. papers d.45 f.93.

William Jones

William Jones, son of Thomas Jones late fishmonger to Oxford University, was apprenticed to George Tonge, Oxford goldsmith, for seven years, being enrolled 5 January 1763.[1] On April 6, 1771, he announced in *Jackson's Oxford Journal* that he was a working goldsmith/jeweller, and that he had opened a shop in High Street opposite Mrs. Jones, fishmonger. She was probably his widowed mother carrying on her late husband's business. In January 1772, he married the only daughter of William Forty, butcher,[2] and their son William was christened October 12, 1772 at St. Michael-at-the-North Gate.

Most of what is known about William Jones, other than his civic activities, is to be found in *Jackson's Oxford Journal*. The year following his marriage he advertised that he would take light gold in payment. December 30, 1775, he advertised that he had opened a new shop at the corner of Western Avenue in front of the Market on the New Parade, High Street. He was offering a reward of one guinea April 25, 1783, for a gold ring with a cypher in hair which had been lost in "Brazen-nose" Lane.

Business apparently was not very good as September 10, 1784, an advertisement appeared instructing persons who were indebted to him to settle with Mr. George Ballachey, attorney-at-law or they would be sued. All claimants were to send in their accounts. Furthermore, the lease of his house and his stock in trade were to be disposed of, and enquiries were to be made to the attorney. As legal matters tend to do, the business moved slowly as over a year passed before an auction sale of his goods was advertised. Thomas Thomson was to hold the sale on October 12 and 13, 1784, at Jones's house on New Parade, High Street.

[1]Graham, *Oxford City Apprentices,* #2255.
[2]*Jackson's Oxford Journal,* January 28, 1772.

All his household furniture, linen and china were to be sold, and catalogues could be obtained from the auctioneer whose premises were in Broad Street.

The next month Jones's entire stock in trade was for sale well under prime cost at his late shop in the High Street. It seems that buyers did not materialize as on January 24, 1785, it was announced that the stock would be sold by Mr. Hales, auctioneer. Also in January the new stone-built freehold dwelling house in front of the New Market, High Street, late in the occupation of Mr. William Jones was for sale or let with enquiries to be made to Mr. James Clarke, mercer, Corn Market.

In March 1786, Jones had a milliner's shop near St. Mary's Church to let, proclaiming that the situation was excellent and the trade extensive. By June of that year he was advertising himself as a goldsmith near St. Mary's Church but informing the public that he had a large assortment of fishing tackle. March 20, 1790, he was still listed as a goldsmith in the High Street.

These advertisements in the *Oxford Journal* give the impression that Jones went bankrupt, sold off his possessions, paid off his creditors, moved up the street and started over. One wonders where his wife figured in the sale of the household goods. It seems that his only employment by the colleges was in 1776 when he was paid £3/0/9 for unspecified work done for Trinity College.[3] He apparently was cast more in the role of a small tradesman rather than an actual working goldsmith.

Jones did, however, take a prominent part in City government. September 30, 1772, he was chosen for a seat on the Common Council. He was sworn November 4, and paid £3/10/0 in lieu of entertainment and 3s. 4d. for not being constable. Two years later he was again on the Common Council, then with the term beginning September 30, 1778 through the 1790 term he was chamberlain.[4]

November 23, 1787, he was appointed to a committee which included George Tonge and Edward Lock, goldsmiths, to visit the Vice-Chancellor of the University to ask him to suppress all matriculated people who were carrying on trades for which they had not been matriculated. When the Council met again on December 10, the Vice-Chancellor had given his reply in which he agreed that no person should be carrying on a trade which was not specified in his matriculation except in businesses which were

[3]Trinity College Computus Bursariorum, I A/5.
[4]OCA, 1752–1801, 98 *et passim*.

143

closely allied such as those of barber and perfumer. The Vice-Chancellor requested a list of the errant tradesmen. Jones was a member of the committee to draw up the list and present it to the Vice-Chancellor.[5]

After 1790, William Jones fades from the records.

[5]*Ibid.*, 184.

Elusive Goldsmiths
and Apprentices

The names of a number of goldsmiths and apprentices appear in the records about whom very little is known. Those apprentices who came from places in the shire outside the City of Oxford may have returned to their respective birthplaces to carry on the craft or may have found opportunities in more remote places. Others may not have completed their apprenticeships. A few master goldsmiths seem to have gone from Oxford almost as mysteriously as they came.

The London Goldsmiths' Company 9 October 1718 fined Mr. Wentworth of Sarum [Salisbury] £5/5/6 for selling substandard gold- and silverwares.[1] Less than two years later, 16 June 1720, **MR. WENTWORTH**, goldsmith of Oxford, was being a problem for the Company.[2] In that year Balliol made an unspecified payment to him,[3] and in 1724 Magdalen paid him £5/7/0.[4] In 1733 Corpus Christi paid him 6s. for exchange of old plate.[5] Jesus, in 1736, paid him 4s. for mending plate and £1/15/0 for a seal-press.[6]

It has been impossible to determine if this is the same Mr. Wentworth who might have migrated from Salisbury to Oxford since no Christian name is employed in either case. It is unlikely, however, that they were one and the same person as Timothy Kent records the first one as Thomas Wentworth who died in 1740 in Salisbury.[7] There is, however, possibly a

---

[1]Goldsmiths' Company Court Minute Book 11, p. 452.

[2]*Ibid.,* 12, p. 73.

[3]Balliol College Liber Bursarii.

[4]Magdalen College Bursar's Book.

[5]Corpus Christi Magni Libri, c/1/1/16.

[6]Jesus College MSS., P.H.1.

[7]T. A. Kent, "Salisbury Silver and Its Makers, 1550–1700," *Silver Society Journal* (1993), III, 50.

family connection. Nothing is known of the origins of the Oxford Mr. Wentworth or of what became of him after 1736 when he disappears from Oxford records. **GEORGE WENTWORTH**, watchmaker and gold-smith of Oxford, took an apprentice in 1720, so it is undoubtedly he who was summoned to Goldsmith's Court in that year, and the Mr. Wentworth who is found in college records.

NICHOLAS ASHCOMBE of St. Michael-at-the-North Gate, Oxford, goldsmith, no age given, was married to Susannah Neighbour, of Worm-ingwall, Buckinghamshire, 7 April 1724, at St. Peter-in-the-East or St. John, Oxford. There is no further record of him.

HODGES HENZELL, goldsmith in the parish of St. Clement, Oxford, 5 April 1743, insured his dwelling house for £160 and his household goods for £40.[8]

RICHARD GOLDWIRE of the parish of St. Clement, Oxford, regis-tered his mark with the London Company. His first mark was entered as a smallworker 28 March 1753, and his second mark 15 September 1763. He was still in Oxford when in the Survey of Oxford in 1772 he was listed as owner or occupier of a house in St. Clement's, and the follow-ing year he appeared in the Parliamentary Report List as Richard Glad-wire, plateworker. He seems to have been first in Salisbury as a snuff box of 1744 is noted with an RG mark and engraved "Richard Gladwyer Sarum."[9] Undoubtedly he was the supplier of boxes to Edward Lock pre-viously discussed.

JAMES SINDREY was granted freedom of the City of Oxford 20 May 1788 on payment of 20 guineas and the usual fees.[10]

FRANCIS KNIGHT is mentioned only a few times. Wednesday, 26 June 1706 he appeared at Goldsmiths' Hall to answer to the Court for Mr. Dubber who was accused of selling goldwares worse than standard.[11] In 1773 Exeter College paid him £8/0/0 for his plate.[12] William Wright, in 1729, took out a Sun Fire Insurance policy for £40 on the backside of a house in St. Aldate's parish occupied by F. Knight, goldsmith.[13] He was married to Anne Roberts April 15, 1711 at St. Aldate's, and buried there

---

[8]London Guildhall 11936, vol. 65, 494.
[9]Grimwade, *London Goldsmiths, 1697–1837*, 723.
[10]*OCA, 1752–1801*, 185.
[11]Goldsmiths' Company Court Minute Book 10, p. 309a.
[12]Exeter College A.II.10.
[13]London Guildhall 11936, vol. 29, n.p.

August 19, 1732. Their son, Francis, was apprenticed to an Oxford cooper April 18, 1735.[14]

RICHARD HICKMAN, son of Edward Hickman of Great Missenden, Buckinghamshire, yeoman, was apprenticed to George Tonge, goldsmith of Oxford, 11 December 1766.[15] Lincoln utilized his services in 1792.[16] June 14, 1779 he and four others were to have £25 of Sir Thomas White's benefaction provided they gave such security as was approved by the House.[17] Hickman insured his timber and slated dwelling house in All Saints parish for £200 May 10, 1806.[18] In 1821 he was employed by Oriel,[19] but this was probably his son.

HENRY OAKLEY HICKMAN, son of Richard Hickman, was apprenticed to his father 9 May 1796; enrolled 8 May 1797.[20] He was baptized 11 June 1782 at All Saints, and was buried 29 January 1822, age 39, apparently at All Saints. His address was given as High Street in the parish of St. Mary's. His parents, Richard and Elizabeth Gurden Hickman, both of All Saints parish, were married there 25 June 1778.

The earliest apprentice of whom little is known was **JOHN GREVELL,** son of John Grevell, gentleman, of North Leigh, Oxfordshire, who was apprenticed to **JOHN PARSON,** 28 September 1592.[21] The master may have been **JOSUA PARSON,** goldsmith, who was admitted to the liberty of the City March 9, 1591,[22] upon payment of 100s. and 4s. 6d.[23] The 100s. payment would indicate he was a "stranger;" i.e., a new arrival in the City. Josua Parsons, late citizen and goldsmith "in ye High Street," was buried at St. Botolph, Aldgate, London, 10 September 1614.[24] Having died intestate, his estate amounting to £68/10/8, was administered by his widow, Benedicta Parsons, in the Archdeaconry Court of London.[25]

---

[14]Graham, *Oxford City Apprentices, 1697–1800*, #1594.

[15]*Ibid.,* #2332.

[16]Lincoln College Calculus.

[17]*OCA, 1752–1801,* 134.

[18]London Guildhall 11937, vol. 66, n.p.

[19]Oriel College Treasurers' Accounts, ETC B2.

[20]Graham, *op. cit.,* #3105.

[21]Hanaster Book, 1590–1614, L.5.1.

[22]*Ibid.*

[23]*OCA, 1583–1626,* 61.

[24]London Guildhall 9222/1.

[25]London Guildhall 9050/5f.45. He is given here as Joshua.

THOMAS WYSE, son of Thomas Wyse of Abingdon, Berkshire, yeoman, was apprenticed to William Wright May 4, 1607.[26] Ten years later, 29 July 1617, THOMAS GREENE, son of Thomas Greene of Marstonficre [Meysey?] in the County of Gloucester, yeoman, was apprenticed to William Wright.[27] October 17, 1657, WILLIAM CHILLINGWORTH, son of Ralph Chillingworth of the City of Oxford, brewer, was apprenticed to William Wright,[28] grandson of the first William Wright. LAWRENCE TAYLOR, son of John Taylor of the City of Oxford, tobacco pipe maker, was apprenticed to Alexander Wright July 5, 1666.[29]

An earlier apprentice was THOMAS BUSBYE, son of John Busbye of the City of Oxford, cordwainer, who was apprenticed to Thomas Crompton, 8 June 1621.[30] THOMAS SAYER, son of Lawrence Sayer, a London goldsmith, was apprenticed on June 25, 1667 to William Robinson.[31] There is no record of his father's apprenticeship under the London Company. On February 17, 1676/7 WILLIAM SALTER, son of William Salter of Hanborough in the County of Oxford, yeoman, was apprenticed to JOSEPH PALMER, a plateworker who does not appear further in the records.[32] Salter apparently returned to Hanborough where he had been baptized January 12, 1650/1, and died there February 12, 1702/3. His father had died in September 1684. On September 10, 1677, CHARLES BADGER, son of John Badger of London, cordwainer, was apprenticed to Richard Dubber.[33]

Moving into the eighteenth century, DOILEY WISE, son of William Wise of Bodicote, Oxfordshire, husbandman, was apprenticed to George Wentworth, watchmaker and goldsmith, 6 August 1720. There is no indication of which trade, or both, that he was to learn.[34] STEPHEN HEDGES, son of William Hedges of Iffley, Oxfordshire, mason, was apprenticed to John Wilkins, Esq., Mayor of Oxford, goldsmith, 21 February 1734/5.[35] He had been baptized May 5, 1717 at St. Mary the Virgin,

[26]Hanaster Book, 1590–1614, L.5.1.
[27]Hanaster Book, 1613–1640, L.5.2.
[28]Hanaster Book, 1639–1662, L.5.3.
[29]*Ibid.*
[30]Hanaster Book, 1613–1640, L.5.2.
[31]Hanaster Book, 1662–1699, L.5.4.
[32]*Ibid.*
[33]*Ibid.*
[34]Graham, *op. cit.,* #1059.
[35]*Ibid.,* #1586.

Iffley. The parish register lists him as the son of William and Sarah Hegis. May 27, 1767 **THOMAS JACKSON,** son of Simmons Jackson late of Oxford, yeoman, deceased, was apprenticed to Edward Lock.[36] **THOMAS TURNER,** son of Elizabeth Turner, was apprenticed to George Tonge, silversmith, 25 February 1774 on payment of £60.[37] He advertised his business as jeweller and goldsmith at the New Parade, High Street, in *Jackson's Oxford Journal* March 29, 1788. On September 30 of that year, the *Journal* noted that he had been elected a chamberlain. Edward Lock took another apprentice, **JOHN DAVIS,** son of Morgan Davis of St. Michael's parish, Oxford, 3 October 1785.[38]

Grimwade lists four Oxford lads who were apprenticed to London goldsmiths. First was **JOHN DANIELS** who was perhaps the son of John Daniel of the City of Oxford, yeoman, who was apprenticed to Robert Finch in 1681 and was free 19 August 1690. **THOMAS MOULDON,** son of Thomas Mouldon, late of Oxford, farmer deceased, was apprenticed to Dru Drury 6 May 1713 on payment of £5/0/0. Five years later he was turned over to John Taylor, watchcase maker, and received his freedom October 5, 1721. **RICHARD MAY,** son of Charles May of the City of Oxford, grocer, was apprenticed to William Dorrell 15 October 1753 on payment of £21/0/0, and was free 14 January 1761. His father, who died in 1761, was macebearer of the City of Oxford. **JOSEPH LOCK,** son of Joseph Lock of the City of Oxford, malster, was apprenticed to John Moore 6 June 1764 on payment of £20. He gained his freedom 7 August 1771. A connection with the Oxford goldsmiths of the same name has not been established. All of these men spent the rest of their lives working in London.

[36] *Ibid.,* #2335.
[37] *Ibid.,* #2492.
[38] *Ibid.,* #2749.

A Last Word

Many different trades were pursued in Oxford over the centuries to supply the local citizenry and University community with the necessities of life, but goldsmithing does not really fall into this category. The distance between Oxford and London is not great, and even in days of slow-moving transportation, there was much going and coming and transporting of goods. For instance, the Chancellor's Court Register in 1528 mentions Thomas Foster as being the University's common carrier.[1] At least two of the colleges had dealings with Richard Gossen, a London goldsmith in the early seventeenth century, and such costly goods were carried in carts along with other merchandise once a week in spite of the ever-present hazard of highwaymen.

Considering this relative ease of movement coupled with the fact that no goldsmiths' guild existed in Oxford, it is rather surprising that the colleges and the University placed such heavy reliance on the local craftsmen. It is extremely rare to find in the accounts payments made to goldsmiths other than those working in Oxford. The earliest extant accounts seem to indicate that Oxford goldsmiths actually *made* the articles purchased by the academic establishment, and in the case of Thomas Berry in the mid-seventeenth century it is a proved fact. As time progressed, however, more and more of their work appears to have been mending, refashioning, gilding and engraving; and, in the eighteenth century, retailing the products of London goldsmiths. Most of the accounts which survive do not precisely differentiate between what has been made by the goldsmith and what he is retailing. The exception to this is John Wilkins II whose bills to Brasenose clearly make the distinction. There are no records, however, of the percentage of markup on goods retailed, but it seems to have been calculated by the ounce. It is definitely known that much work was commissioned, but it is not known how many purchases were made from a

---

[1] Calendar Chancellor's Court Register EEE, 1527–45; 1557, Part I, 1527–1535, f83r.

goldsmith's stock by the University, the colleges and the City with the exception of the quantity of silver boxes purchased by the University from Edward Lock. Nothing can be known of the business carried on with the individual townspeople beyond gold rings, silver bodkins and spoons.

It is not possible to evaluate the skill of the Oxford goldsmiths as practically nothing of their work survives with the exception of engraving, and in this the best of them excelled. Some of the work which is presumed to have been made locally is definitely crude. The University and the colleges tended to use a single goldsmith for the duration of his life and then one of his family members. Those not so favoured were not so prosperous. Such employment was not necessarily a measure of skill, however, as other factors such as politics and nepotism must be considered.

The Oxford goldsmiths were a varied and interesting lot and not always law-abiding. Some came from well-established families; some did not. It is to be sorely regretted that no corpus of their work survived the ravages of the Civil War and the melting pot of later generations.

Appendix

Three Staves and a Badge

The Staves

Oxford has never been recognized as a center of the goldsmith's craft, yet there were nearly one hundred goldsmiths in the City from the later Middle Ages to 1800. By the early fourteenth century the London Company of Goldsmiths were making ordinances applicable to the provinces regarding the marking of plate and searches for goods wrought from silver of less than sterling standard (92.5 fine).[1] Oxford goldsmiths seem to have ignored the legislation, and the Goldsmiths' Company Court Minute Books reveal that no official searches were ever made in Oxford. In the eighteenth century, though, a few of the City's goldsmiths were brought before the Court for selling substandard goods and were fined.

The ravages of the Civil War, improper care, and refashioning resulted in the loss of nearly everything produced by Oxford goldsmiths. Four objects, however, survive in the Ashmolean Museum which are almost certainly the work of local craftsmen; i.e., three University staves and a University Marshal's badge. None bear hallmarks or makers' marks. Manuscripts in the University Archives, although lacking in some essential facts, do throw light on the origin of these splendid relics of an earlier time.

On July 7, 1566, the Chancellor wrote, "The Queen is coming to Oxford; make preparations for her reception." Two days later it was decided that the expenses of her visit should be paid by the "Custodes clavium" [?Keeper of the Keys].[2] Vivian Green of Lincoln College wrote in *The Illustrated History of Oxford University* (1993) that the three University staves which are now in the Ashmolean Museum were purchased for the Queen's visit, but no document seems to exist authorizing the purchase of them. This hardly seems plausible since she arrived in August thus

[1]*Cal. Patent Rolls, 1327–1330*, 42–43.
[2]Andrew Clark, *Reg. of the Univ. of Oxford*, II, part I, 234.

making for a very short time for any goldsmith to produce three staves. They *were* made in 1566 as shown by the accounts of the Vice-Chancellor, Dr. John Kennall. The University paid £59/6/8 for them, but it is most unfortunate that the name of the goldsmith is not stated.[3]

A close examination of the staves leads to the conclusion that they were locally made as the work appears to be too crude to have been produced in a London workshop. If, in fact, they *were* ordered after notice of the Queen's impending visit was received, it would have been imperative that a local goldsmith be employed. The only known possibility is Thomas Gowre [or Gower] who was admitted to the freedom of the City in 1565/6, and was known to be doing business with the University in 1569.[4]

Little more than a year after the staves were made the bedels were evidently complaining that they were too heavy as on 9 December 1567, a committee was appointed to consider the weight of the staves before the beginning of next Term.[5] This is not surprising as although of a not unduly thick guage of silver sheets which are wrapped around a wooden core, the heads are large fluted iron cones, reminiscent of the days when a stave was also a weapon. It appears that the bedels' complaints were ignored.

Nothing more is recorded regarding the staves until the Parliamentary Visitors in 1647 discovered them missing, and became determined to find them. It was so important to the Visitors that they be found because the staves represent the authority of the University, and Parliament was intent on seizing that authority. On 4 April 1648 they signed a warrant for breaking into the lodgings of the President of Corpus Christi College, Dr. Newlin. Coming up empty-handed from their search, two days later the Visitors demanded that the staves be delivered into their hands. That failing, they next ordered 3 October 1648 that the revenues derived from certain lectures be used to buy new staves for the bedels. This was ignored as on 28 December, after threatening to have the bedels arrested for carrying off the University goods, an order was issued promising immunity to further molestation if by 14 January they would deliver the staves to the Vice-Chancellor. This, too, was ignored. On 18 September 1649, the Visitors, giving up the notion that the staves were going to be found, or-

---

[3]University Archives, WPB/21/4.

[4]W. H. Turner, *Selections from the Records of the City of Oxford, 1509–1583*, 104, and Clark, *op. cit.*, 338–339.

[5]Clark, *op. cit.*, 260.

dered the colleges to contribute money for purchasing replacements. This obviously also was ignored.[6]

Where they had been hidden probably always will remain a mystery, but it was not long before they surfaced. In 1650–1652, Samuel Wilkins, a local goldsmith, was paid 13s. 2d. for mending the bedels' staves several times.[7] The following year [1653–1654] the University paid Mr. Wright [either Martin or William II] £4/8/0 for mending and new gilding the staff belonging to the Superior Bedel in Divinity.[8] Thomas Berry in 1656–1657 was paid 10s. for mending Mr. Langley's staff[9] [Medicine and the Arts]. No more repairs were made until 1668–1669 when Mr. Collier's staff was mended, and in 1671–1672, 10s. was paid to Samuel Wilkins for mending Mr. Ball's staff.[10]

The repairs continued. In 1688–1689, the Vice-Chancellor notes, "Paid Mr. Wilkins for mending Mr. Colier, the Bedel's staff. 15s."[11] This would have been John Wilkins the Elder. He was paid £1/0/0 for mending the bedels' staves in 1710–1711, and the following year the cost for repairs was 10s. In 1713–1714, Mr. Thistlethwayte's staff needed mending, but no amount paid nor the name of the goldsmith is listed.[12] Chances are that it was John Wilkins.

The University finally gave up on the old staves and bought new ones in 1723, undoubtedly through John Wilkins, but made by Benjamin Pyne, a London goldsmith. Local goldsmiths frequently acted as retailers. The accounts for 1722–1723 show a payment of £177/4/6 to Wilkins, and the following year £91/19/6.[13] The first payment would have been for the staves for the superior bedels. These are larger than those of the inferior bedels and were gilt. The smaller ones are silver with only the tops gilt.

The staves represent the three faculties of Divinity, Medicine and the Arts, and Law, and each, old and new, are decorated with the motto appropriate to each faculty in large raised letters. Of the old staves the top plate of two of them is engraved with the arms of the University, the open

[6]Montague Burrows, *Register of the Visitors of the University of Oxford, 1647–1658,* 7, 18, 19, 200, 214, 262.
[7]University Archives, WPB/21/4.
[8]*Ibid.*
[9]*Ibid.*
[10]WPB/21/5.
[11]*Ibid.*
[12]WPB/21/6.
[13]*Ibid.*

book being inscribed, *In principio erat verbum et verbum erat apud Deum,* the opening words of St. John's Gospel which was the University motto at that time. The top plate of the other one is engraved with the Royal Arms of the House of Tudor. The decoration of the shaft on one stave is different from that on the other two. Rather than arabesques it is engraved with a small imbricated leaf design. It is possible that this one was made by a different goldsmith, especially when considering the brief time allowed for their manufacture if indeed made after the announcement of the impending royal visit. There is also the possibility that this stave was already in existence when the other two were made. Unlike the others, the shaft has been broken and mended with a silver band. The Vice-Chancellor's account does not specify the number of staves for which payment was made. The Latin entry, *Solut pro conficiendii Baculi sive insignibus Bedellorii* translates *Paid for procuring staves or insignia for the Bedels.*

The two staves with identical decoration on the shafts were found in 1895 in a long-undisturbed box on the top of a tall case in the University Archives. The third was in the keeping of the Esquire Bedel until that office ceased to exist, then it was taken to the University Chest.

From the record of repairs it seems fairly certain that the staves came out of hiding shortly after the Parliamentary Visitors gave up hope of finding them and dropped the matter. In the accounts of 1650–1652, Wilkins was paid 13s. 2d. for mending them *several* times. This implies that *all* the work may not have been done during that accounting period. Some of the colleges were often as much as three years in arrears in payments to goldsmiths, and this may well have been true of the University, especially in this time of turmoil. These various repairs are very evident on the staves.

Benjamin Pyne, before making the six new staves in 1723, must surely have made sketches of the old ones as it is obvious that a conscious effort was made to reproduce the principal elements of design found on the ancient staves. It is also possible that the sketches were done by John Wilkins and sent to Pyne. This design must have been the will of the University as Pyne was noted for his civic and church regalia and would not have been lacking in originality.

The flat ends, or plates, are engraved with coats-of-arms and it is probable that the engraving was the work of John Wilkins. It seems to have been rather customary for London goldsmiths who filled Oxford orders to send up the finished products with coats-of-arms to be engraved by local goldsmiths. In this case the stave of the Superior Bedel of Divinity bears the arms of Montague and Monthermer quartered with a difference for Nevill rather than the arms of the University as on the old one. The University arms with the current motto, *Dominus illuminatio mea,* are on three of the six, while one is engraved with the arms of the House of Stuart, and one with the old Plantagenet arms of the House of Tudor.[14] The armorial engraving of these three plates or roundels seems to be in a seventeenth century style, which adds to the presumption that the engraving was *not* done by Benjamin Pyne. Perhaps Wilkins copied the arms from some earlier examples he had at hand. This, however, does not explain the choice of the Neville-Montague arms which appear to be the arms of George Neville, Archbishop of York and Chancellor of the University in 1455.[15] There is a possibility that the use of these ancient arms was meant to denote a continuity of the authority of the University from before the Reformation.

The Marshal's Badge

The badge which was sewn on the left sleeve of the distinctive coat worn by the University Marshal, who was also known as the Bedel of the Beggars, is on loan to the Ashmolean from the University Church of St. Mary the Virgin. In the Vice-Chancellor's Accounts of 1694–1695, £2/0/0 was paid to the Marshal for a badge.[16] It apparently was left to him to procure it. Four years later payment of £2/8/8 was made to the "Bedell of Beggars for a coate and a Badge."[17] For being made of silver the badge would appear to have had a short life, and the very next year (1700–1701) the supposed new badge was mended, and again in 1703–1704.[18] The badge must have had better care in succeeding years, as it was not until 1735–1736 that further mention is made of it when Wilkins was paid 1s.

---

[14]Described in H. C. Moffatt, *Old Oxford Plate,* 4–7.

[15]I am indebted to Ted East, former University Marshal, and John Dobson, University Verger, for some of this information, and to Mr. Dobson for making it possible for me to handle the 1723 staves; and, to Timothy Wilson, Keeper of the Department of Western Art, Ashmolean Museum, for allowing me to handle the ancient staves.

[16]WPB/21/5.

[17]WPB/21/6.

[18]*Ibid.*

Staves of the Faculties of Law, Theology, and Medicine and the Arts. Copyright Ashmolean Museum, Oxford. Reproduced with permission.

Detail of head of stave. Copyright
Ashmolean Museum, Oxford. Reproduced with permission.

161

Detail of University Arms on end of stave. Copyright Ashmolean Museum, Oxford. Reproduced with permission.

for cleaning and mending it. He mended it again in 1740–1741, and the following year the mending cost 1s. 6d.[19]

It is unfortunate that the accounts do not indicate who made the badge, but it is certainly of local workmanship. Measuring 12.5 cm. × 16.4 cm., it weighs approximately 6 oz. 3 dwt. Oval in shape, the repoussé coat-of-arms of the University is surmounted by leafy scrolls. The open book is very angular and gives only a hint that there are pages in the book. The

[19]WPB/22/1.

Marshal's Badge, Ashmolean Museum. On loan from the University Church of St. Mary the Virgin. Reproduced with permission.

engraved motto, *Dominus illuminatio mea,* is so badly spaced that the words are not properly aligned and extra space is left at the end. A flange around the outer edge of the border of husks is punched with holes for sewing the badge to the coat sleeve.

The reverse side is crudely scratched with *RR* and *Richard Payd[e].* These may refer to the names of two of the Marshals who wore the badge. More significant, though, is the fact that the five mends enumerated in the Vice-Chancellor's Accounts are clearly visible.

In analyzing the accounts it appears that the entry of 1699–1700 must be in error. Why would a new badge be necessary after only four years unless the one purchased in 1694–1695 had been lost or that the Marshal had pocketed the £2/0/0 paid him instead of buying a badge, both of which seem unlikely. It will be recalled that the payment made in 1699–1700 was £2/8/8, the alleged cost of both coat and badge, but in 1706–1707 the cost of only a new coat for the Marshal was £2/7/0[20], and in 1694–1695, the cost of the badge was £2/0/0. The payment in 1699–1700 was more likely to have been for *mending* the badge rather than for a new one. The conclusion can be drawn that a new badge was not purchased, and the one on display is that of 1694–1695.

The only question remaining is, "Who was the maker?" This cannot be answered conclusively, but there is little doubt that it was John Wilkins the Elder. The first Wilkins employed by the University was his father, Samuel, in 1650–1652. He died in 1688/9. Wright is mentioned once and Thomas Berry once; otherwise, a Wilkins was the University goldsmith up to 1758, the year of the death of John Wilkins II, nephew of John the Elder who died in 1727.

The 1723 staves are still in use, and the Marshal's badge in use today is a 1910 copy of the one in the Ashmolean.

[20]WPB/21/6.